THIS ~~BOOK~~ BELONGS to:
JOURNEY

_____

DAte:

_____

A YEAR OF WEEKS

Running Press
Hachette Book Group
1290 Avenue of the Americas, New York, NY 10104
www.runningpress.com
@Running_Press

Printed in China

First Edition: April 2021

Published by Running Press, an imprint of Perseus Books, LLC,
a subsidiary of Hachette Book Group, Inc. The Running Press name and logo
is a trademark of the Hachette Book Group.

The Hachette Speakers Bureau provides a wide range of authors
for speaking events. To find out more, go to www.hachettespeakersbureau.com
or call (866) 376-6591.

The publisher is not responsible for websites (or their content)
that are not owned by the publisher.

Design direction by Frances J. Soo Ping Chow.

Library of Congress Control Number: 2020944214

ISBNs: 978-0-7624-9912-0 (hardcover), 978-0-7624-9911-3 (e-book)

RRD-S

10 9 8 7 6 5 4 3 2

A YEAR OF WEEKS

52 AWESOME WEEKS OF
TRYING NEW THINGS

erica root.

Running Press
PHILADELPHIA

<u>ABOUT</u> this <u>ADVENTURE</u>.

THE NEXT 52 WEEKS are ALL ABOUT TRYING things YOU'VE NEVER TRIED, EXPLORING YOUR CREATIVE SIDE, LEARNING to <u>LOVE</u> YOURSELF MORE and MORE, and TONS OF OTHER INCREDIBLE THINGS. FEEL FREE to COMPLETE EACH TOPIC in ORDER or JUMP AROUND the BOOK— REMEMBER, this is (YOUR) JOURNEY and <u>YOU</u> GET to DECIDE HOW to NAVIGATE! BUT MOST IMPORTANTLY, BE OPEN to the EXPLORATION... and <u>HAVE</u> <u>FUN</u>!

weather today:
HIGH 64° F
low 51° F
RAINY
BEST PART of MY DAY:
DINNER with FRIENDS...
A WEEK of DAILY LOGS
HAPPY
EXCITED!
NERVOUS
TODAY I am so thankful for:
THE SOUND of the OCEAN WAVES

KEEPING a LOG of your DAY CAN HELP you REMAIN present AND mindful BY REMINDING you to PAY ATTENTION to the WAY you ARE FEELING and the THINGS that FILL your DAY. LET'S GET STARTED!

Fill in the shapes and write in the information about your day.

DAY 1 /date: _____

WEATHER:
LOW TEMP: _____   HIGH TEMP: _____

WATER: 1 2 3 4 5 6 7 8

BEST PART of MY DAY: _____
_____
_____

MOOD:

SOMETHING I'M GRATEFUL FOR:
_____

NOTES: _____
_____

DAY 2 /date: _____

WEATHER:
LOW TEMP: _____   HIGH TEMP: _____

WATER: 1 2 3 4 5 6 7 8

BEST PART of MY DAY: _____
_____
_____

MOOD:

SOMETHING I'M GRATEFUL FOR:
_____

NOTES: _____
_____

DAY 3 / date: _____

WEATHER:

☀️ ⛅ ☁️ 🌧️ ⚡ ⛄

LOW TEMP: _____   HIGH TEMP: _____

WATER: 1 2 3 4 5 6 7 8

BEST PART of MY DAY: _____
_____
_____

MOOD: 😄 🙂 😐 😕 ☹️ 😢

SOMETHING I'M GRATEFUL FOR:
_____

NOTES: _____

DAY 4 / date: _____

WEATHER:

☀️ ⛅ ☁️ 🌧️ ⚡ ⛄

LOW TEMP: _____   HIGH TEMP: _____

WATER: 1 2 3 4 5 6 7 8

BEST PART of MY DAY: _____
_____
_____

MOOD: 😄 🙂 😐 😕 ☹️ 😢

SOMETHING I'M GRATEFUL FOR:
_____

NOTES: _____

DAY 5 / date: _____

WEATHER:

☀️ ⛅ ☁️ 🌧️ ⚡ ⛄

LOW TEMP: _____   HIGH TEMP: _____

WATER: 1 2 3 4 5 6 7 8

BEST PART of MY DAY: _____
_____
_____

MOOD: 😄 🙂 😐 😕 ☹️ 😢

SOMETHING I'M GRATEFUL FOR:
_____

NOTES: _____

"the best part of my day was..."

WEEKEND LOG

DAYS 6-7/dates: _____

BEST WEATHER DAY this WEEKEND: (SAT.) (SUN.)

low temp: _____   high temp: _____

BEST meal:

FAVORITE Activity:

PEOPLE I SPENt time With:

this WEEKEND I FELt MOStLY:

BECAUSE:

SOME things I am GRATEFUL for this WEEKEND:

A WEEK OF
TRYING NEW THINGS

USE THIS WEEK to TRY SOME NEW THINGS AND DECIDE on SOME THINGS YOU'D LIKE TO TRY in the FUTURE.

TRY a NEW FOOD

INTRODUCE YOURSELF to SOMEONE YOU'VE BEEN NERVOUS to TALK to.

TEACH YOURSELF HOW to SEW.

SIGN UP FOR a COOKING CLASS

THINK of 3 THINGS YOU'LL TRY this WEEK and 3 THINGS YOU'LL TRY in the FUTURE. WRITE THEM DOWN HERE:

THIS WEEK I'LL TRY:

DAY 1

date: _____

WHAT I TRIED: _____
HOW WAS IT? _____
_____
_____
WILL I DO IT AGAIN? ☐ YES ☐ NO

DAY 2

date: _____

WHAT I TRIED: _____
HOW WAS IT? _____
_____
_____
WILL I DO IT AGAIN? ☐ YES ☐ NO

DAY 3

date: _____

WHAT I TRIED: _____
HOW WAS IT? _____
_____
_____
WILL I DO IT AGAIN? ☐ YES ☐ NO

 **BOOK CLUB**

 **TRY a NEW RECIPE**

 **LEARN ABOUT ASTROLOGY**

SOME THINGS I'LL TRY SOON:

DAY 4 date: _____	I'M GOING to TRY: _____ _____ DATE I'D LIKE to DO it BY: _____ ☐ I TRIED it!! HOW WAS it? _____ _____ WOULD I DO it AGAIN? ☐ YES ☐ NO
DAY 5 date: _____	I'M GOING to TRY: _____ _____ DATE I'D LIKE to DO it BY: _____ ☐ I TRIED it!! HOW WAS it? _____ _____ WOULD I DO it AGAIN? ☐ YES ☐ NO
DAYS 6/7 date: _____	I'M GOING to TRY: _____ _____ DATE I'D LIKE to DO it BY: _____ ☐ I TRIED it!! HOW WAS it? _____ _____ WOULD I DO it AGAIN? ☐ YES ☐ NO

A WEEK OF

FLOWERS

PICK a DIFFERENT FLOWER
EACH DAY to LEARN ABOUT
and DRAW.

Choose flowers from the list on
the next page - or come up with
your own.

FLOWERS:

PEONY LILAC

WAXFLOWER

LAVENDER MUM

DAHLIA ASTER

ANEMONE IRIS

CASPIA FREESIA

HEATHER ROSE

SNAPDRAGON

LILY of the VALLEY

they do best in partial shade

Scientific Name:
CONVALLARIA MAJALIS

they don't do well in hot weather.

DRAW it HERE ↘

DAY 1/date: ———————

FLOWER: ————————————

SCIENTIFIC NAME:

————————————————————

NOTES: —————————————

————————————————————

DAY 2 /date: _____
FLOWER: _____
  SCIENTIFIC NAME:

_____

NOTES: _____
_____
_____

DAY 3 /date: _____
FLOWER: _____
  SCIENTIFIC NAME:

_____

NOTES: _____
_____
_____

DAY 4 /date: _____
FLOWER: _____
  SCIENTIFIC NAME:

_____

NOTES: _____
_____
_____

DAY 5 / date: _____
FLOWER: _____
 SCIENTIFIC NAME:
_____
NOTES: _____
_____
_____

DAYS 6-7 / date: _____
FLOWER: _____
SCIENTIFIC NAME:
_____
NOTES: _____
_____
_____

THE EARTH LAUGHS IN FLOWERS. —RALPH WALDO EMERSON

A WEEK of COMPLIMENTS

> I really love that hat!

> Oh, thank you! I knitted it myself.

SPEND this week making OTHERS feel good by COMPLIMENTING them. PAY SPECIAL attention to THINGS you LIKE or ADMIRE and LET THEM KNOW!

DAY	WHO?	HOW'D it GO?
DAY 1 date:___		
DAY 2 date:___		
DAY 3 date:___		
DAY 4 date:___		
DAY 5 date:___		
DAYS 6-7 date:___		

A WEEK OF drinking enough water

Some facts about water:

1. WATER HELPS CLEANSE YOUR BODY INSIDE and OUT.

2. DRINKING ENOUGH WATER HELPS YOUR SKIN LOOK its BEST.

3. STAYING HYDRATED CAN HELP BUILD and REPAIR MUSCLES.

TRACK your WATER this WEEK

EACH TIME YOU DRINK AT LEAST 6 oz. OF WATER, FILL IN ONE OF THE SHAPES.

1 2 3 4 5 6 7 8

DAY 1 / date: _____

DAY 2 / date: _____

1 2 3 4 5 6 7 8

DAY 3 / date: _____

1 2 3 4 5 6 7 8

1 2 3 4 5 6 7 8

DAY 4 / date: _____

1 2 3 4 5 6 7 8

DAY 5 / date: _____

1 2 3 4 5 6 7 8

DAY 6 / date: _____

1 2 3 4 5 6 7 8

DAY 7 / date: _____

YOU DID IT!

a week of IMPORTANT and INSPIRATIONAL PEOPLE

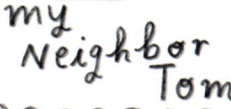

my Neighbor Tom

Grandma Rose

Mrs. Kim—my 2nd grade teacher

THIS WEEK THINK ABOUT the PEOPLE THAT are IMPORTANT to YOU and INSPIRE YOU. MAYBE THEY'RE FRIENDS, FAMILY, CELEBRITIES, or FAMOUS HISTORICAL FIGURES. BRIEFLY WRITE WHAT MAKES them IMPORTANT to YOU, then DRAW a PICTURE of THEM.

DAY 1 / date: _____
this is _____.
why they're amazing:
_____
_____
_____.

← this is _____
_____.

DAY 2
date: _____ they're so
amazing because: _____
_____
_____.

DAY 3 / date: _____
this is _____.
they're amazing because:
_____
_____
_____.

DAY 4 / date: _____
this is _____.
why they're amazing:
_____
_____
_____.

←this is _____
_____.

DAY 5
date: _____ they're so
amazing because: _____
_____
_____.

DAYS 6-7/date: _____
this is _____.
they're amazing because:
_____
_____
_____.

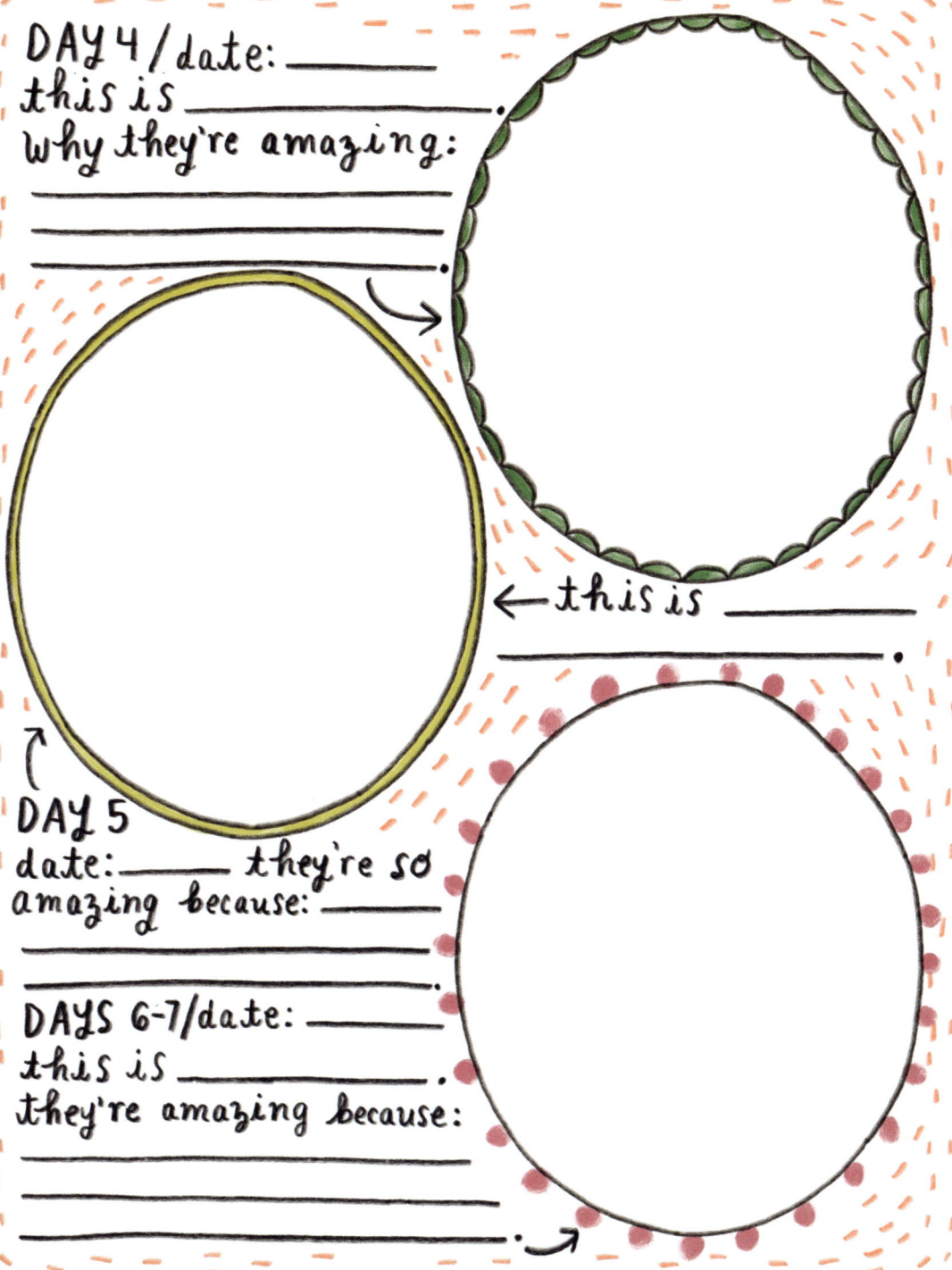

DECORATE the BOOKMARKS HOWEVER
YOU WANT: PATTERNS, ANIMALS, FLORALS...
THERE ARE REALLY NO RULES and NO
LIMITS THIS WEEK. JUST HAVE FUN!
KEEP them ALL or GIVE SOME AWAY.

tip: ONCE YOU'VE DECORATED and
CUT OUT YOUR BOOKMARKS, COVER with
CLEAR PACKING TAPE on BOTH SIDES,
and CUT AROUND the EDGES→DIY
LAMINATION!

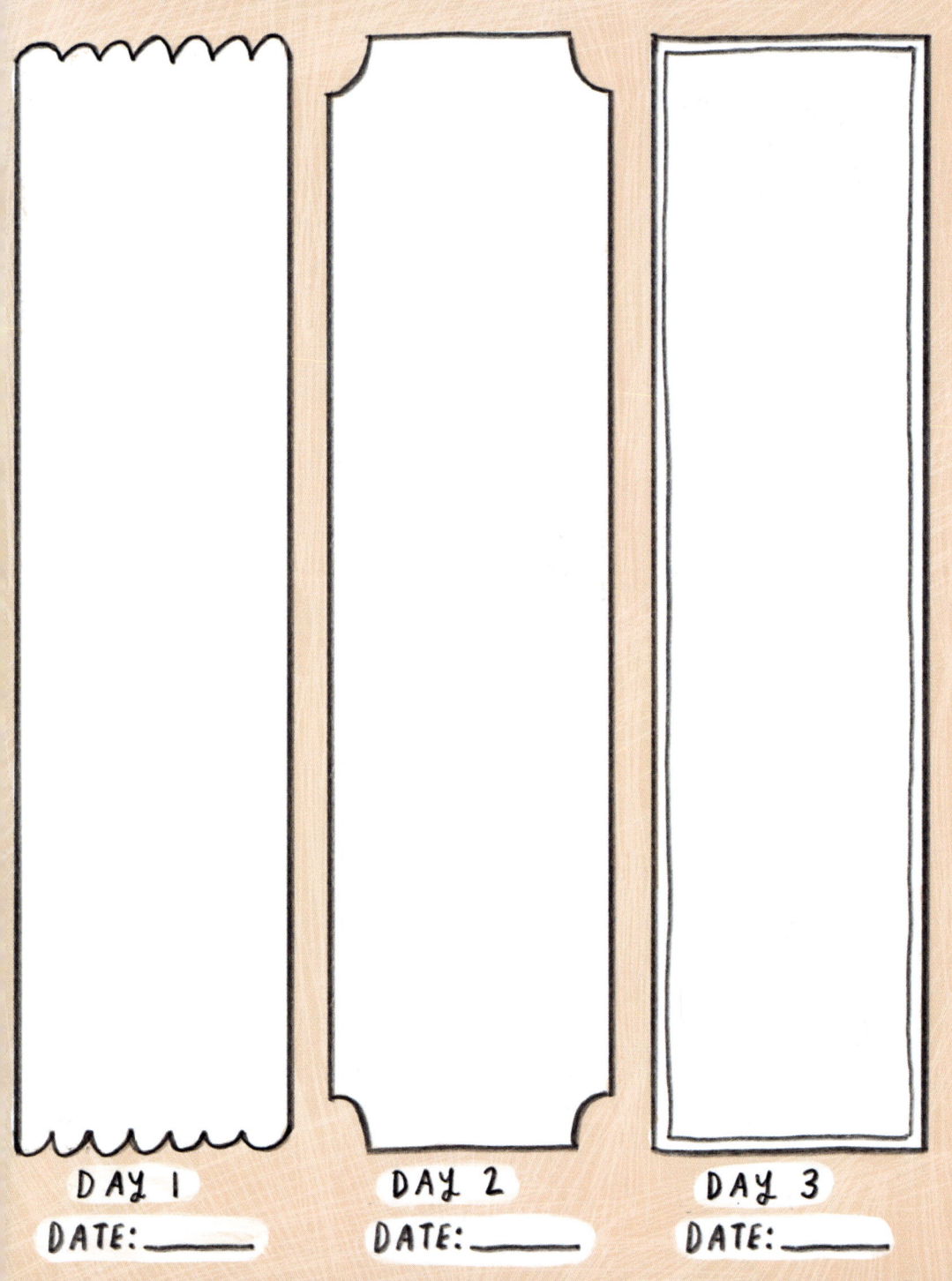

DAY 1

DATE: _____

DAY 2

DATE: _____

DAY 3

DATE: _____

DON't FORGEt to DECORAtE the BACKS.
then... CUT us out!

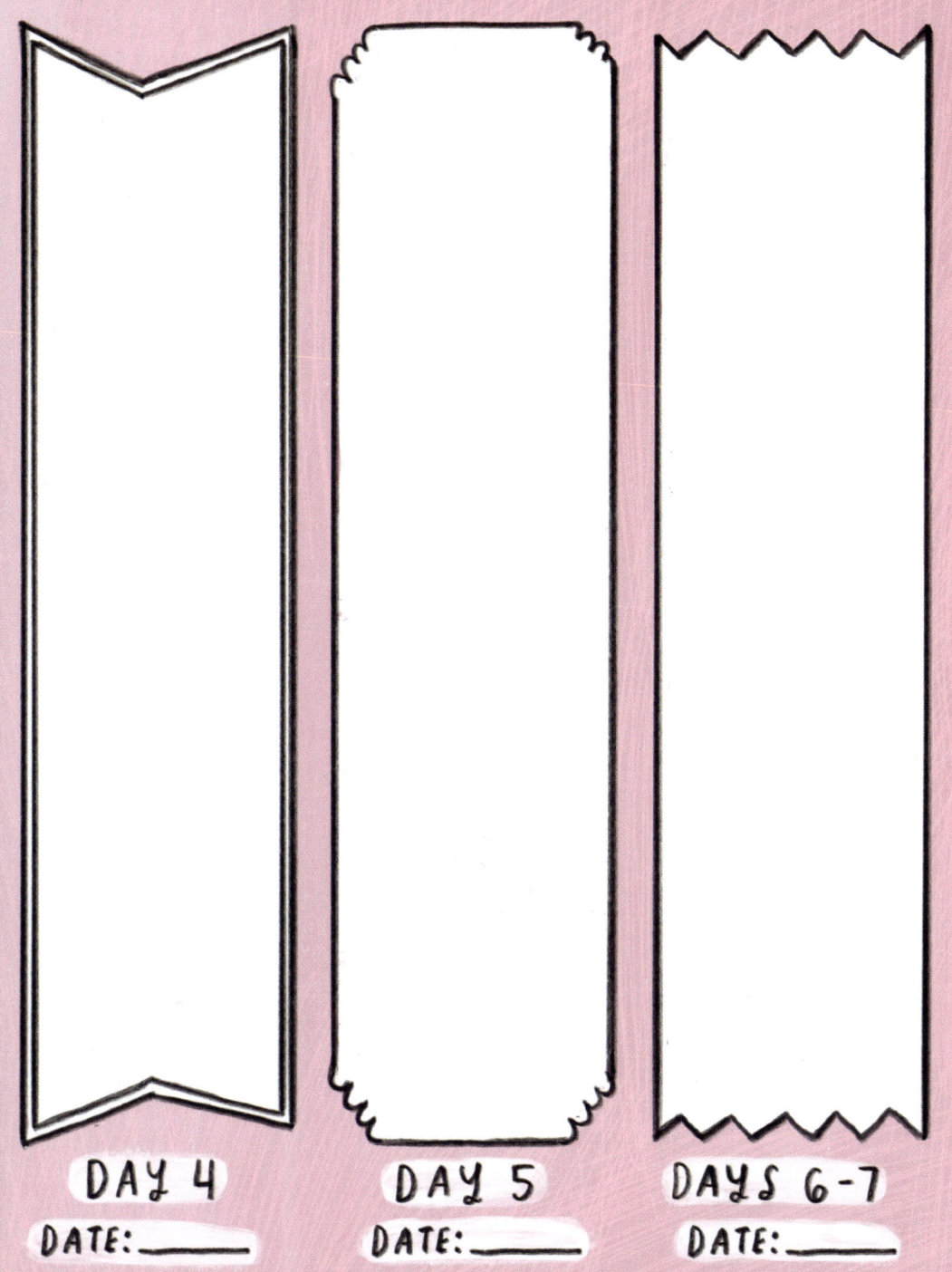

DAY 4

DATE:_____

DAY 5

DATE:_____

DAYS 6-7

DATE:_____

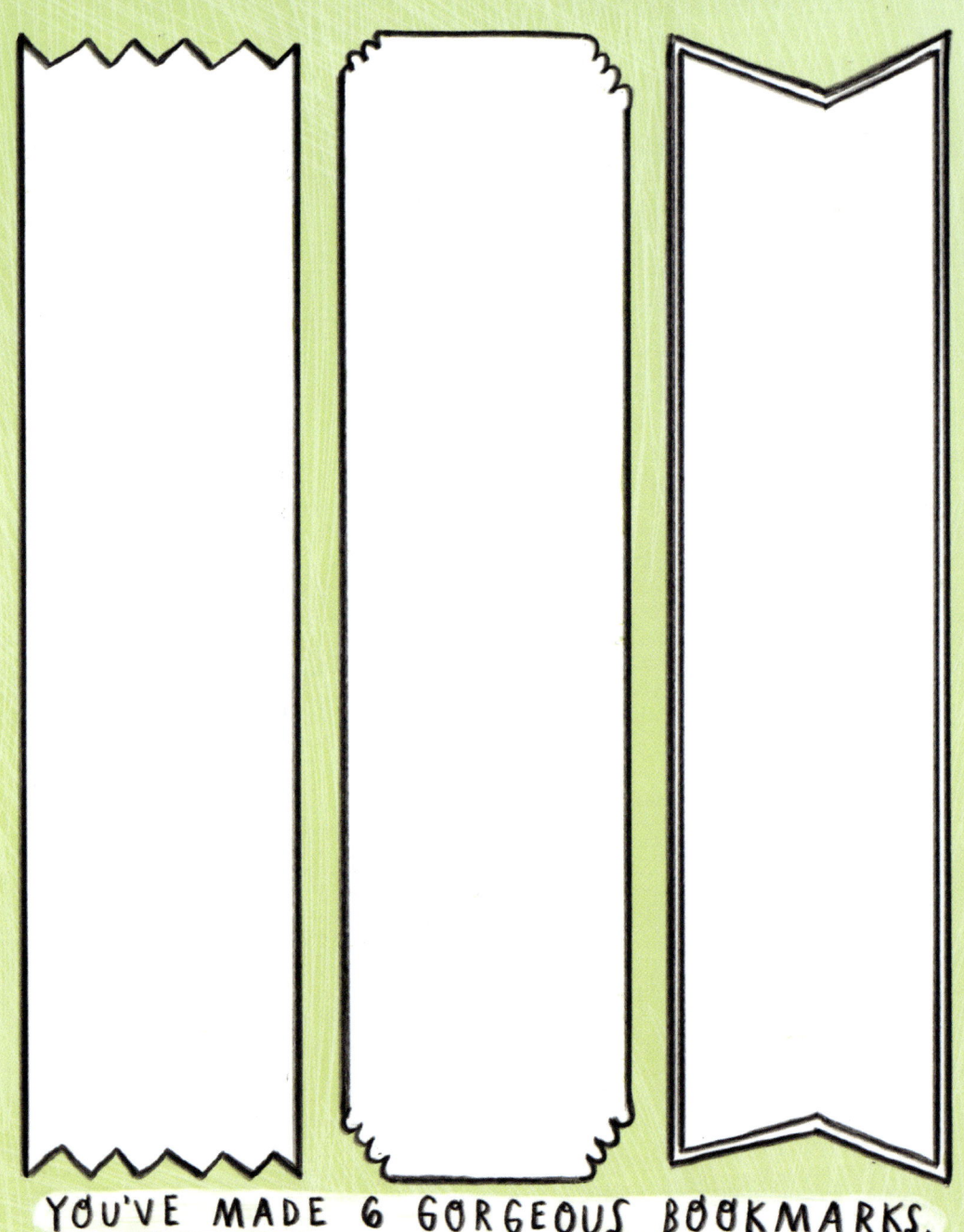

YOU'VE MADE 6 GORGEOUS BOOKMARKS, NOW GO FIND A BOOK and PUT them to USE!

A WEEK OF LESS TECH TIME

TECHNOLOGY HAS IMPROVED OUR LIVES in SO MANY WAYS, BUT if WE ALLOW it to, TECHNOLOGY CAN ALSO DISCONNECT US FROM the WORLD and the PEOPLE AROUND US. THIS WEEK RECONNECT with LIFE BEYOND a SCREEN!

- ⊙ WAKE UP + ENJOY a CUP OF TEA/COFFEE BEFORE LOOKING at YOUR PHONE.
- ⊙ DELETE YOUR SOCIAL MEDIA APPS for a DAY.
- ⊙ DON'T LOOK at YOUR PHONE in BED at NIGHT.
- ⊙ EAT a MEAL WITHOUT WATCHING T.V. OR GOING on YOUR PHONE.
- ⊙ INSTEAD of PULLING OUT YOUR PHONE to TAKE a PHOTO/VIDEO, JUST APPRECIATE the MOMENT.
- ⊙ RESIST the URGE to BRING YOUR PHONE into the BATHROOM.

CHOOSE FROM the LIST ABOVE (or pick your own) TO START CUTTING BACK ON TECH TIME. WHAT DID YOU DO and HOW DID it MAKE YOU FEEL?

☐ DAY 1 / date: _____

☐ DAY 2 / date: _____

☐ DAY 3 / date: _____

☐ DAY 4 / date: _____

☐ DAY 5 / date: _____

☐ DAYS 6-7 / date: _____

SOME SELF-LOVE IDEAS:

- BUY YOURSELF FLOWERS

- LOOK IN the MIRROR and SAY three POSITIVE things ABOUT YOURSELF. (they don't HAVE to BE PHYSICAL things.)

- BE gentle WITH YOURSELF. HOW do you TALK to YOURSELF? ARE you kind. PATIENT, UNDERSTANDING? TALK to YOU the WAY you WOULD talk to YOUR FRIENDS.

- RESPECT YOUR BOUNDARIES. SAY NO when YOU KNOW YOU SHOULD. DON'T take on TOO MUCH!

- ALLOW OTHERS to COMPLIMENT YOU. INSTEAD of DIS- AGREEING, JUST Say "THANK YOU." YOU are WORTH the COMPLIMENTS!

- WRITE DOWN a FEW things YOU are PROUD of or HARD times THAT YOU WERE ABLE to PULL YOURSELF through. REMIND your- SELF HOW BRAVE and POWERFUL you ARE!

- TAKE time FOR YOU... take a BATH BY CANDLELIGHT, READ a BOOK, GO to YOUR FAVE restaurant.

JOURNAL

CHOOSE FROM the IDEAS on the PREVIOUS PAGE or COME UP WITH YOUR OWN IDEAS to FOCUS on this WEEK. PICK ONE (or MORE) to DO EACH DAY. JOT DOWN WHAT YOU DID and HOW it MADE YOU FEEL. ♥

DAY 1/date: ⎯⎯⎯⎯⎯⎯

DAY 2/date: ⎯⎯⎯⎯⎯⎯

DAY 3/date: ⎯⎯⎯⎯⎯⎯

DAY 4/date: ⎯⎯⎯⎯⎯⎯

DAY 5/date: ⎯⎯⎯⎯⎯⎯

DAYS 6-7/date: ⎯⎯⎯⎯⎯⎯

A WEEK OF MINDFULNESS

I AM LIVING in this EXACT MOMENT.

I AM AWARE of MY OWN PRESENCE.

I WILL SIT WITH MY EMOTIONS BEFORE RESPONDING to THEM.

I FEEL the EARTH UNDER MY FEET.

But what EXACTLY is MINDFULNESS??

MERRIAM-WEBSTER DEFINITION:

mindfulness (noun)

\ˈmīn(d)-fəl-nəs\ | mind·ful·ness

1. the quality or state of being mindful

2. the practice of maintaining a nonjudgmental state of heightened or complete awareness of one's thoughts, emotions, or experiences on a moment-to-moment basis

AH, OKAY — SO BASICALLY IT'S ALL ABOUT BEING REALLY AWARE of the FEELINGS and EMOTIONS of RIGHT NOW.

SOME MINDFULNESS EXERCISES

WHEN EATING A MEAL, CLOSE YOUR EYES and NOTICE the TEXTURES and FLAVORS of the FOOD. CHEW SLOWLY and ENJOY EACH BITE.

WHEN YOU WAKE UP, INSTEAD of GETTING OUT of BED to START YOUR MORNING ROUTINE, PRACTICE MINDFULNESS. BECOME AWARE of YOUR BREATHS. FEEL the BLANKETS on YOUR BODY. STRETCH OUT YOUR ARMS and LEGS and BRING YOUR FULL ATTENTION to this MOMENT and DECIDE to CONTINUE this DAY WITH PURPOSEFUL INTENTION.

WHEN YOU TAKE a SHOWER, PAY CLOSE ATTENTION to the WAY the WATER FEELS on YOUR BODY. TRY to FEEL the WARMTH of EACH DROP.

FIND a QUIET SPOT. SIT DOWN WITH YOUR FEET on the FLOOR. SIT SILENTLY and NOTICE EACH PART of YOUR BODY: the WAY the FLOOR FEELS on the BOTTOM of YOUR FEET, the SOUND of YOUR BREATH, the RISE and FALL of YOUR CHEST, the WARMTH of YOUR OWN BODY HEAT. NOTICE HOW it FEELS to BE ALIVE RIGHT at this MOMENT.

MY WEEK of MINDFULNESS

DAY 1 / date: _____

how it made me feel:

WHAT I TRIED: ———
_____
_____

WAS it EASY or
CHALLENGING?
(FILL in YOUR ANSWER)

① ② ③ ④ ⑤ ⑥ ⑦ ⑧ ⑨ ⑩

CHALLENGING   EASY

DAY 2 / date: _____

how it made me feel:

WHAT I TRIED: ———
_____
_____

WAS it EASY or
CHALLENGING?
(FILL in YOUR ANSWER)

① ② ③ ④ ⑤ ⑥ ⑦ ⑧ ⑨ ⑩

CHALLENGING   EASY

DAY 3 / date: _____

how it made me feel:

WHAT I TRIED: ———
_____

WAS it EASY or
CHALLENGING?
(FILL in YOUR ANSWER)

① ② ③ ④ ⑤ ⑥ ⑦ ⑧ ⑨ ⑩

CHALLENGING   EASY

MY WEEK of MINDFULNESS
(CONTINUED)

DAY 4 / date: _____

how it made me feel:

WHAT I TRIED: _____
_____
_____

WAS it EASY or CHALLENGING?
(FILL in YOUR ANSWER)

① ② ③ ④ ⑤ ⑥ ⑦ ⑧ ⑨ ⑩

CHALLENGING   EASY

DAY 5 / date: _____

how it made me feel:

WHAT I TRIED: _____
_____
_____

WAS it EASY or CHALLENGING?
(FILL in YOUR ANSWER)

① ② ③ ④ ⑤ ⑥ ⑦ ⑧ ⑨ ⑩

CHALLENGING   EASY

DAYS 6-7 / date: _____

how it made me feel:

WHAT I TRIED: _____
_____

WAS it EASY or CHALLENGING?
(FILL in YOUR ANSWER)

① ② ③ ④ ⑤ ⑥ ⑦ ⑧ ⑨ ⑩

CHALLENGING   EASY

A WEEK OF BIRDS

Each day this week, choose a different bird from the list (or pick your own). Write its common _and_ scientific names, _and_ draw a picture.

NIGHTINGALE
SKYLARK WEAVER
CRANE WARBLER
EMU KIWI HOOPOE
MACAW QUAIL
PARROT MYNA

Scientific Name: (SPHENISCIDAE)

PENGUIN

there are currently 18 species of Penguin.

THEIR WINGS have (EVOLVED) into FLIPPERS!

PENGUINS have KNEES but they ARE HIDDEN BENEATH their FEATHERS.

DAY 1 / date: _____
BIRD NAME _____
_____ (common)
_____
(scientific)

DAY 2 / date: _____
BIRD NAME _____
_____ (common)
_____
(scientific)

BIRD PARTS:

tail feathers
wing
crown
cheek
throat
breast
belly
foot

DAY 3 / date: _____
BIRD NAME _____
_____ (common)
_____
(scientific)

DAY 4 / date: _____

BIRD NAME _____
_____ (common)

_____
(scientific)

DAY 5 / date: _____

BIRD NAME _____
_____ (common)

_____
(scientific)

DAYS 6-7 / date: _____

BIRD NAME _____
_____ (common)

_____
(scientific)

BIRDHOUSES and FEEDERS.

A WEEK OF FOLLOWING A Morning Routine

GOOD MORNING!

Let's make a PLAN!

BEING ORGANIZED and IN CONTROL of your MORNING is a GREAT WAY to START the DAY with POSITIVITY.

WRITE DOWN the THINGS you'd LIKE to do WHEN you START EACH DAY. USE SOME IDEAS from this LIST or COME UP with OTHERS that WORK BEST for you.

SOME MORNING ROUTINE IDEAS...

- DRINK a GLASS of WATER
- STRETCH for 5 MINUTES
- SHOWER
- EAT BREAKFAST
- REVIEW the DAY'S SCHEDULE
- PACK LUNCH

- MAKE the BED
- FEED / WALK PET(S)
- DO SOME BREATHING EXERCISES
- GO FOR a RUN
- SIT and ENJOY a CUP of COFFEE / tea
- JOURNAL or SKETCH

(WEEKDAYS)

MY MORNING ROUTINE:

_____
_____
_____
_____
_____
_____
_____
_____
_____
_____
_____
_____
_____

(WEEKENDS)

MY MORNING ROUTINE:

_____
_____
_____
_____
_____
_____
_____
_____

★ DEPENDING on HOW tight YOUR ROUTINE NEEDS to BE, YOU CAN EVEN WRITE the TIME that EACH iTEM ON YOUR LiST SHOULD take PLACE.

★ IF YOUR WEEKDAY ROUTiNE iS DiFFERENT FROM YOUR WEEKEND ROUTINE, WRiTE a SEPARATE LiST FOR EACH.

YOU'VE GOT THIS!

DAY 1 / date: _____

☐ Routine Completed!

Notes: _____

_____

_____

DAY 2 / date: _____

☐ Routine Completed!

Notes: _____

_____

_____

DAY 3 / date: _____

☐ Routine Completed!

Notes: _____

_____

_____

DAY 4 / date: _____

☐ Routine Completed!

Notes: _____

_____

_____

DAY 5 / date: _____

☐ Routine Completed!

Notes: _____

_____

_____

DAYS 6-7 / date: _____

☐ Routine Completed!

Notes: _____

_____

_____

WHY STOP NOW?!

You are awesome!

KEEP it UP!

a week of
FINDING BEAUTY
in the ORDINARY

BEAUTY is ALL AROUND US. SOMETIMES WE GET SO BUSY that WE MISS IT. SPEND this WEEK FOCUSING on the BEAUTY that SURROUNDS YOU EVERY DAY. IT DOESN'T HAVE to BE MONUMENTAL to BE BEAUTIFUL. A STRANGER HELPING SOMEONE. THE WAY the SUN is SHINING THROUGH the WINDOW. THE COLOR of a FALLEN FLOWER PETAL AGAINST the SOIL. FIND at LEAST ONE THING EACH DAY and WRITE it HERE. GETTING in the HABIT of NOTICING ORDINARY BEAUTY MAKES US MORE APPRECIATIVE of EVEN the SMALLEST THINGS.

the sound of the rain on the window.

the way this mom looked at her child on the bus.

the way the leaves fell off the tree.

DAY/date	BEAUTY in the ORDINARY
DAY 1 date: _____	TODAY I NOTICED:
DAY 2 date: _____	TODAY I NOTICED:
DAY 3 date: _____	TODAY I NOTICED:
DAY 4 date: _____	TODAY I NOTICED:
DAY 5 date: _____	TODAY I NOTICED:
DAYS 6-7 date: _____	TODAY I NOTICED:

A WEEK OF BREAKFASTS

DRAW YOUR BREAKFASTS this WEEK!

DAY 1 / date: _____
TODAY'S breakfast: _____
_____
_____
_____

DAY 2 / date: _____
TODAY'S breakfast: _____
_____
_____
_____

DAY 3 / date: _____

TODAY'S breakfast: _____

_____

_____

DAY 4 / date: _____

TODAY'S breakfast: _____

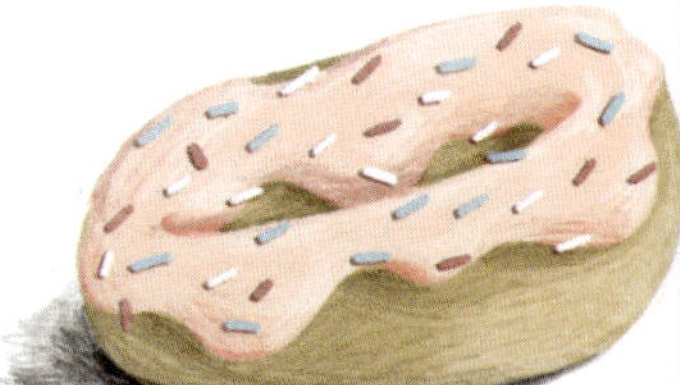

_____

DAY 5 / date: _____
TODAY'S breakfast: _____
_____

DAYS 6-7 / date: _____
TODAY'S breakfast: _____
_____

A WEEK OF THINGS I WANT TO SEE and DO

LEARN to SWIM.

CHECK OUT the NEW LOCAL DONUT SHOP!

LEARN how to SKATE.

SEE Mt. FUJI.

DRAW SOME things YOU WANT to SEE or DO
in EACH BOX.

DAY 1 / date: _____
I WANT TO : _____
_____

DAY 2 / date: _____
I WANT TO : _____
_____

DAY 3 / date: _____
I WANT TO: _____

DAY 4 / date: _____
I WANT TO: _____

DAY 5 / date: _____
I WANT TO: _____

DAYS 6-7 / date: _____

I WANT TO: _____

CHOOSE :ONE: that YOU WANT to DO _this_
YEAR and START a PLAN!

THIS YEAR I WILL: _____

THINGS I NEED _in_ ORDER _to_ MAKE _it_ HAPPEN:

☐ _____ ☐ _____
☐ _____ ☐ _____
☐ _____ ☐ _____

ACTION STEPS:

① _____ ④ _____
② _____ ⑤ _____
③ _____ ⑥ _____

A WEEK OF Quotes

WHEN YOU COME ACROSS a QUOTE that's REALLY SPECIAL to YOU it CAN MOTIVATE YOU, BRING YOU PEACE, or LIFT YOUR SPIRITS WHEN YOU NEED it MOST. BY the END of this WEEK YOU'LL HAVE three BEAUTIFUL QUOTES to HANG UP, CARRY in YOUR BAG, or SHARE WITH a FRIEND.

SOME HELPFUL tips:

- A SIMPLE ONLINE SEARCH WILL BRING YOU a TON OF WONDERFUL QUOTES to CHOOSE FROM.

- IN ORDER to AVOID DAMAGING YOUR QUOTE CARDS, "LAMINATE" them on BOTH SIDES WITH SOME PACKING TAPE.

DAY 1 / date: _____

FIND a QUOTE that REALLY SPEAKS to YOU. DON'T WORRY ABOUT MAKING it LOOK NICE... YOU'LL do that TOMORROW.

QUOTE: _____
_____
_____
_____
_____

SAID BY:
_____

DAY 2 / date: _____

REWRITE the QUOTE FROM YESTERDAY HERE → then CUT it OUT.

DON'T FORGET to WRITE WHO the QUOTE is BY here

DAY 3 / date: _____

FIND ANOTHER QUOTE that is SPECIAL to YOU. AGAIN, don't WORRY ABOUT MAKING it LOOK NICE... YOU'LL do that TOMORROW.

QUOTE: _____
_____
_____
_____
_____

SAID BY:
_____

I KNOW WHERE I'M GOING and I KNOW the TRUTH, and I DON't HAVE to BE WHAt YOU WANt ME to BE. I'M FREE to BE WHO I WANt.

— MUHAMMAD ALI

when you reach the end of your rope, tie a knot in it and HANG ON.

— FRANKLIN D. ROOSEVELT

CUT OUT and CARRY it FOR WHEN YOU NEED SOME EXTRA ENCOURAGEMENt or POSITIVITY.

KEEP Your FACE ALWAYS TOWARD the ☼SUNSHINE☼ and the SHADOWS WILL FALL BEHIND YOU.

— WALT WHITMAN

DAY 4/date:_____

REWRITE the QUOTE
FROM YESTERDAY HERE →
then CUT it OUT.

DON't FORGEt
to WRITE
WHO the
QUOTE is BY
here

DAY 5/date:_____

QUOTE:_____

FIND ANOTHER
MEANINGFUL QUOTE.
DON't WORRY ABOUt
MAKING it LOOK PRETTY...
YOU'LL do that TOMORROW.

SAID BY:

DAYS 6-7/date:_____

REWRITE the QUOTE
FROM YESTERDAY HERE →
then CUT it OUT.

DON't FORGEt
to WRITE
WHO the
QUOTE is BY
here

BELIEVE YOU CAN and YOU'RE HALFWAY theRE.
—THEODORE ROOSEVELT

the journey of a thousand miles begins with one step.
—LAO TZU

CUT OUt YOUR QUOtES and HANG them UP AROUND YOUR ROOM, ON the BATHROOM MIRROR, PUt ONE in YOUR WALLEt, or EVEN GIVE ONE to A FRIEND!

the BEST PREPARATiON for TOMORROW is DOiNG YOUR BESt today.
—H. JACKSON BROWN JR.

a week of

DRAWING
mugs

DAY 1 /date: _____
DESIGN this ONE ⟩

florals

CREATE YOUR OWN here ⤴

DAY 2 /date: _____

ANIMALS
DESIGN this ONE ⤵

⤶ CREATE YOUR OWN here

DAY 3 / date: _____

FACES

DESIGN *this* ONE↘

DRAW YOUR OWN *here*↗

DAY 4 / date: _____

foods

DRAW YOUR OWN FOOD mug HERE↘

← DESIGN *this* ONE

DAY 5/date: _____

DRAW YOUR OWN here ↘

TATTOOS

tAttOO this MUG ↗

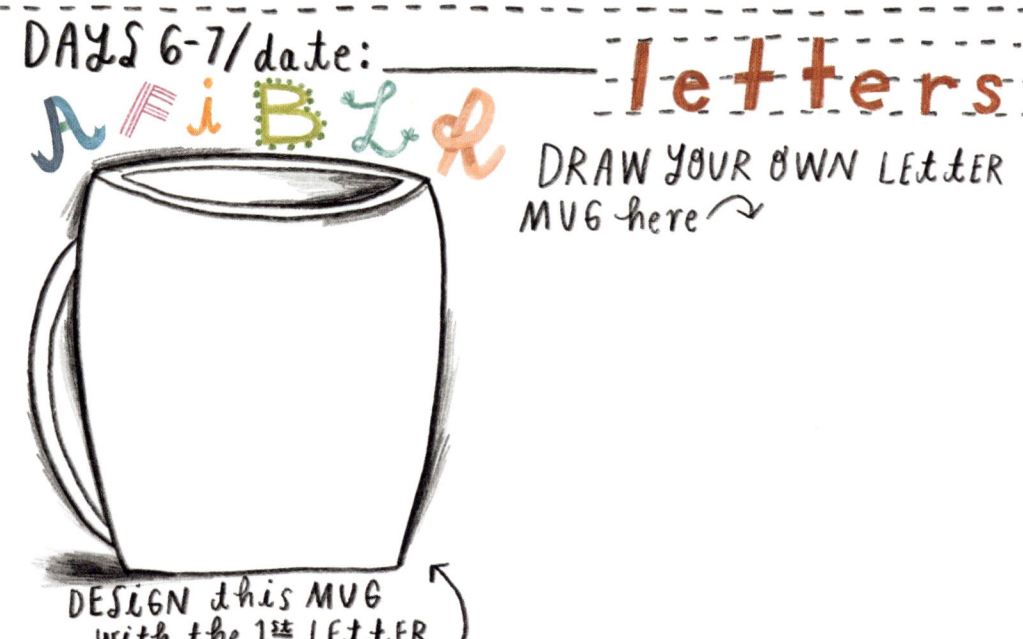

DAYS 6-7/date: _____

letters

DRAW YOUR OWN LETTER MUG here ↩

DESIGN this MUG with the 1st LETTER OF YOUR NAME ↩

A WEEK OF
CLEANING UP Small SPACES

VS.

Clutter and an overabundance of "stuff" can really make us feel uncomfortable in our own homes. This week is all about taking small steps to organize and declutter your space.

*TIP: PURCHASE CLEANING PRODUCTS THAT are MULTI-PURPOSE. YOU WILL NEED LESS STORAGE SPACE for THEM and it WON'T BE as TRICKY to FIND the RIGHT ONE FOR the JOB.

PAPERWORK

DAY 1 | date : _____

SORT MAIL, receipts, and PAPERWORK into FOUR PILES:

1. trash 2. RECYLE
3. SHRED 4. file

*DON'T WAIT-FILE NOW!

YOU GOT THIS!

RECEIPT

stickers—2.00

HOW DID I DO?

HOW CAN I KEEP IT UP?

DUSTY CORNERS

DAY 2 | date : _____

DUST loves to hide in CORNERS!

GO AROUND and SWEEP them all...

"BYE, DUSTBALLS!"

☐ SWEEP all CORNERS

☐ DO A LITTLE DUST-DANCE!

☐ SET A REMINDER TO DO this AGAIN EACH MONTH!

DATE I CHOSE : _____

DAY 3 / date: _____

LET IT GO

DO I really NEED these?

good meowning

WOULD SOMEONE else use this MORE than ME?

FIND :5: things THAT YOU NO LONGER WANT or NEED and **LET THEM GO!** (DONATE IF YOU CAN!)

I GOT RID OF:

1. _____

2. _____   3. _____

4. _____   5. _____

WILL I REALLY use THIS?

DAY 4 / date: _____

BOOKS

GO THROUGH YOUR BOOKS and CHOOSE

10 to GIVE to A FRIEND or to YOUR LOCAL LIBRARY!

favorite book:

_____

most RECENTLY READ:

_____

NEXT, I WANT to READ: _____

DAY 5/date: _____ *dishes*

DISH SOAP

the **DISHES**

WASH

and

CLEAN *out* the **SINK.**

- ☐ DISHES WASHED
- ☐ SINK CLEANED
- ☐ BIG SMILE

DAYS 6-7/date: _____ C L O S E T

LOOK in YOUR CLOSET. FIND the CLOTHES

YOU HAVE not WORN WITHIN

the PAST 12 MONTHS.

AND DONATE them! LETTING GO feels AWESOME!

MOST RIDICULOUS ITEM OF CLOTHING FOUND: _____

OF *things* I DONATED _____

A WEEK OF APPRECIATING NATURE

MAKE an EFFORT to NOTICE the NATURAL WORLD AROUND YOU. EVEN if it is AS SMALL as a BEAUTIFUL LEAF or the WAY the RAIN DROPS SOUND on the ROOF. EACH DAY DRAW WHAT it is YOU NOTICED BELOW and on the NEXT PAGE.

A WEEK OF DESIGNING
home decor

DESIGN the ITEMS that YOU'D LOVE to OWN. IS YOUR style FOLKSY? WACKY? traditional? ECLECTIC? GO AS WILD or LAID BACK as YOU'D LIKE with YOUR PATTERNS.

DAY 1
date: _____

DAY 2 / date: _____

DAY 3
date: _____

DAY 4
date: _____

A WEEK OF HABIT training

THINK of a HABIT YOU'D LIKE to BREAK – or a GOOD HABIT YOU'D LIKE to START. WRITE it HERE:

Habit: ______________________

CHECK OFF a BOX EACH DAY YOU DIDN'T DO YOUR BAD HABIT – or DID DO YOUR NEW, GOOD ONE!

DAY 1/date: ______	DAY 2/date: ______	DAY 3/date: ______
Notes ______	Notes ______	Notes ______
DAY 4/date: ______	DAY 5/date: ______	DAYS 6-7/date: ______
Notes ______	Notes ______	Notes ______

A WEEK OF MAKING LISTS

KEEPING ORGANIZED LISTS OF TASKS and INFORMATION CAN REALLY HELP YOU FEEL in CONTROL. LISTS are the PERFECT WAY to STAY on TOP OF THINGS to DO and A QUICK and EASY WAY to ACCESS IMPORTANT DATA.

DIRECTIONS:

- EACH DAY MAKE a NEW LIST.
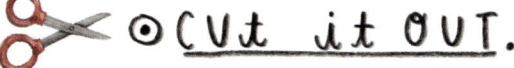 - CUT it OUT.
- HANG it UP or FILE AWAY FOR WHEN YOU NEED to ACCESS it.

LISTS are:
- ☑ helpful
- ☑ beautiful
- ☑ FUN!

WEEKDAY CHORE SCHEDULE

MONDAY:

TUESDAY:

WEDNESDAY:

THURSDAY:

FRIDAY:

FAVE WAYS to RELAX

1

2

3

4

IMPORTANT PHONE NUMBERS

FRIENDS + FAMILY:

MEDICAL / HEALTH

OTHER:

THINGS that MAKE me HAPPY

1.
2.
3.
4.
5.
6.

☑ DAILY to-dos

AM TO-DOS

☐ ☐ ☐ ☐ ☐

PM TO-DOS

☐ ☐ ☐ ☐ ☐

IMPORTANT DATES to REMEMBER

event	date

CONTINUOUS CONTOUR LINE ART

LINE DRAWING

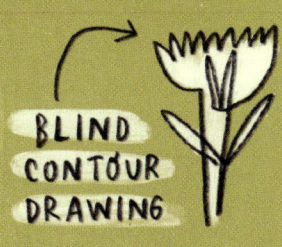

BLIND CONTOUR DRAWING

A WEEK OF

contour drawing

CONTOUR DRAWING is A GREAT WAY to ELIMINATE the FEAR OF NOT BEING ABLE to DRAW SOMETHING. BY LOOKING AT OBJECTS SIMPLY AS LINES and SHAPES YOU ARE ABLE to DRAW the FORM RATHER than ATTEMPTING to DRAW the WHOLE OBJECT, WHICH CAN FEEL a BIT OVERWHELMING.

here we go →

WE'LL FOCUS ON 3 TYPES OF DRAWINGS: ① CONTOUR ② CONTINUOUS CONTOUR ③ BLIND CONTOUR

1. CONTOUR

JUST DRAW the MAIN OUTLINE and the DETAILS that STAND OUT the MOST.

just the most basic and essential lines.

2. CONTINUOUS CONTOUR

YOU'LL FOLLOW the SAME IDEA AS YOU DID WITH REGULAR CONTOUR DRAWING BUT YOU WON'T PICK YOUR PEN/PENCIL OFF the PAGE the ENTIRE TIME.

your pencil stays on the paper the whole time

3. BLIND CONTOUR

THIS ONE'S JUST LIKE the CONTINUOUS CONTOUR EXCEPT NO LOOKING AT YOUR DRAWING! ONLY LOOK AT the OBJECT YOU ARE DRAWING. YOU CAN LOOK DOWN AT WHAT YOU DREW WHEN YOU'RE ALL FINISHED!

pencil stays on the paper and NO PEEKING till the end!

PICK OBJECTS AROUND the HOUSE to DRAW EACH DAY.

DAY 1 / date: _____
(CONTOUR)

DAY 2 / date: _____
(CONTINUOUS CONTOUR)

DAY 3 / date: _____
(BLIND CONTOUR)

CHOOSE SOME OBJECTS FROM YOUR KITCHEN to DRAW (FRUIT, APPLIANCES, VEGGIES, YOUR SNACK...).

DAY 4/ date: _____

(CONTOUR)

DAY 5/ date: _____

(CONTINUOUS CONTOUR)

DAYS 6-7/ date: _____

(CHOOSE YOUR FAVORITE CONTOUR TYPE)

A WEEK OF GIFT IDEAS

CREATING A LIST OF GIFT IDEAS AHEAD OF TIME HELPS to ELIMINATE STRESS WHILE ALLOWING YOU to FOCUS ON the PEOPLE YOU LOVE INSTEAD!

EACH DAY FOCUS ON A DIFFERENT PERSON OR EVENT AND JOT DOWN SOME GIFT IDEAS. THEY CAN BE HANDMADE PRESENTS, ACTIVITIES TO DO, OR STORE-BOUGHT ITEMS.

DAY 1 /date:_____

NAME: _____
OCCASION: _____
DATE: _____
GIFT IDEAS / NOTES:

_____
_____
_____
_____
_____
_____
_____
_____
_____

DAY 2 /date:_____

NAME: _____
OCCASION: _____
DATE: _____
GIFT IDEAS / NOTES:

_____
_____
_____
_____
_____
_____
_____
_____
_____

DAY 3
date:_____

NAME: _____
OCCASION: _____
DATE: _____
GIFT IDEAS / NOTES:
_____
_____
_____
_____
_____
_____

DAY 4 / date:_____

NAME: _____
OCCASION: _____
DATE: _____
GIFT IDEAS / NOTES:
_____
_____
_____
_____
_____
_____

DAY 5 / date : _____
NAME: _____   OCCASION: _____
DATE : _____   GIFT IDEAS / NOTES: _____
_____
_____
_____
_____

DAYS 6-7/ date : _____
NAME: _____   OCCASION: _____
DATE : _____   GIFT IDEAS / NOTES: _____
_____
_____
_____

DRAW a NEW HAIRSTYLE EACH DAY.

DAY 1   date: _____

DAY 2   date: _____

DAY 3   date: _____

DAY 4   date: _____

ways to MEDITATE

① <u>GUIDED MEDITATION</u>: GUIDED MEDITATION IS GREAT FOR BEGINNERS. THERE are TONS OF FREE RESOURCES ONLINE.

② <u>FOCUSED ATTENTION MEDITATION</u>: THIS TYPE OF MEDITATION has YOU FOCUS ON ONLY ONE THING. IT CAN BE AN EXTERNAL OBJECT LIKE a VASE OR INTERNAL LIKE a SPECIFIC BODY PART OR VISUALIZATION. ANY TIME YOU FEEL DISTRACTED JUST RECENTER YOUR ATTENTION to YOUR CHOSEN FOCUS OBJECT.

③ <u>METTA MEDITATION</u> (<u>LOVING KINDNESS MEDITATION</u>): WHILE SITTING in a COMFORTABLE POSITION, CLOSE YOUR EYES. TRY to CREATE POSITIVE and LOVING EMOTIONS FOR YOURSELF. THEN, THINK OF OTHERS in YOUR LIFE and VISUALIZE that YOU ARE SENDING them PEACE and KINDNESS. IMAGINE SENDING these FEELINGS to SOMEONE YOU'VE had a DISAGREEMENT WITH. A KIND HEART is AN OPEN HEART.

PRACTICE DIFFERENT WAYS to MEDITATE this WEEK OR FOCUS ON ONE TYPE to GET BETTER AT ALL WEEK LONG.

DAY 1

date: _____

MEDITATION I DID TODAY:

_____
_____
_____

HOW I FELT BEFORE MEDITATING:

_____
_____

HOW I FELT DURING and AFTER MEDITATING: _____

_____
_____

DAY 2

date: _____

MEDITATION I DID TODAY:

_____
_____
_____

HOW I FELT BEFORE MEDITATING:

_____
_____

HOW I FELT DURING and AFTER MEDITATING: _____

_____
_____

DAY 3

date: _____

MEDITATION I DID TODAY:

_____
_____
_____

HOW I FELT BEFORE MEDITATING:

_____
_____

HOW I FELT DURING and AFTER MEDITATING: _____

_____
_____

DAY 4

date: _____

MEDITATION I
DID TODAY:

_____

_____

_____

HOW I FELT BEFORE MEDITATING:

_____

_____

**HOW I FELT DURING and AFTER
MEDITATING:** _____

_____

_____

DAY 5

date: _____

MEDITATION I
DID TODAY:

_____

_____

_____

HOW I FELT BEFORE MEDITATING:

_____

_____

**HOW I FELT DURING and AFTER
MEDITATING:** _____

_____

_____

DAYS 6-7

date: _____

MEDITATION I
DID TODAY:

_____

_____

_____

HOW I FELT BEFORE MEDITATING:

_____

_____

**HOW I FELT DURING and AFTER
MEDITATING:** _____

_____

_____

a week of
Outfits

‹today's outfit ›

DAY 1 OutFit / date: _____

DAY 2 OutFit / date: _____

DAY 3 OutFit / date: _____

DAY 4 OUtFit / date: _____

DAY 5 OUtFit / date: _____

DAYS 6-7 OUtFit(s)/ date: _____
(DRAW 1 outfit you WORE - or DRAW BOTH!)

A WEEK of STRETCHING your BODY

FINDING TIME to STRETCH EACH DAY MIGHT SOUND TRICKY at FIRST, BUT EVEN 5 MINUTES a DAY is WAY BETTER than NONE! PLUS, it WILL FEEL so GOOD TO KNOW that YOU ARE USING that TIME to do SOMETHING REALLY POSITIVE for YOUR BODY!

SPOILER. ALERT. YOU WILL love HOW this MAKES YOU FEEL!

STRETCHES

BUTTERFLY STRETCH	KNEES to CHEST STRETCH	SEATED FORWARD BEND	STANDING FORWARD BEND
STANDING QUAD STRETCH	SIDE OBLIQUE STRETCH	CRESCENT POSE	KNEELING QUAD STRETCH
WALL CALF STRETCH 1	WALL CALF STRETCH 2	TRICEPS STRETCH	SHOULDER STRETCH

Choose 5 (or more) of the above stretches to do each day.

7 DAY STRETCHING checklist

☐ DAY① - date: _____   ☐ DAY④ - date: _____

☐ DAY② - date: _____   ☐ DAY⑤ - date: _____

☐ DAY③ - date: _____   ☐ DAYS⑥-⑦ - date: _____

you've done it + your body is so happy right now!
GOOD JOB!

Making the needs of your body a priority isn't just good for for your physical health – it's also great for your mental health to put YOU 1ST!

SOOOO...

SAY THIS OUT LOUD:

I AM WORTH IT!

Try stretching 1ST thing in the morning to start your day feeling healthy and refreshed!

OUCH
ALWAYS = STOP!

Stretching shouldn't hurt! If it's uncomfortable or if you feel pain... STOP!

Stretching is good for EVERY BODY but can be super important if you sit for a large part of your day.

DON'T FORGET ABOUT US!

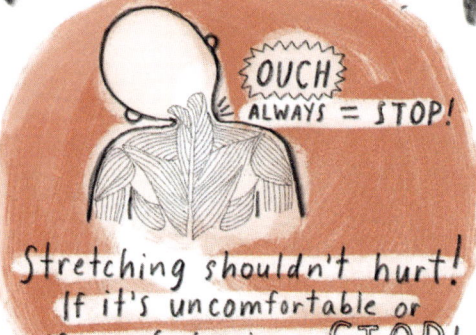

Check in with your body throughout the day. If you feel tight or tense, just take a minute to stretch.

A WEEK OF: DOING ORDINARY THINGS IN NEW WAYS

Day 1 / Date: _____

BRUSH YOUR TEETH WITH YOUR NON-DOMINANT hand.

CHECK OFF WHEN COMPLETE: ☐

Day 2 / Date: _____

take a NEW ROUTE to a PLACE YOU FREQUENTLY VISIT.

CHECK OFF WHEN COMPLETE: ☐

Day 3 / Date: _____

CHECK OFF WHEN COMPLETE: ☐

LISTEN to a NEW PODCAST or artist TODAY.

Day 4 / Date: _____

Loquat

TRY A NEW food today.

CHECK OFF WHEN COMPLETE: ☐

Day 5 / Date: _____

SWITCH UP YOUR MORNING DRINK... have tea INSTEAD OF COFFEE (or anything DIFFERENT).

O.J.

CHECK OFF WHEN COMPLETE: ☐

Days 6-7 / Date: _____

WEAR a DIFFERENT COLOR than YOU TYPICALLY WEAR!

CHECK OFF WHEN COMPLETE: ☐

A WEEK OF
VOLUNTEER
and
CHARITY
ideas

GENEROSITY of YOUR TIME, ITEMS, and RESOURCES NOT ONLY HELPS those IN NEED BUT CAN ALSO REMIND YOU HOW GOOD it FEELS to SPREAD POSITIVITY and to DO the RIGHT THING!

WHAT CAN I DO TO HELP?

THERE are SO MANY GROUPS and ORGANIZATIONS that WOULD LOVE YOUR HELP! DO a QUICK SEARCH ONLINE FOR VOLUNTEER OPPORTUNITIES in YOUR AREA. WHAT'S IMPORTANT to YOU? LIBRARIES? ANIMALS? the ENVIRONMENT? THERE ARE COUNTLESS WAYS to BE SUPPORTIVE in YOUR COMMUNITY. FIND 6 WAYS that YOU'D LIKE to HELP and WRITE them DOWN ON the NEXT PAGES.

DAY 1 / date: _____
VOLUNTEER / CHARITY IDEA: _____
WEBSITE / CONTACT: _____
HOW CAN I HELP?   STEPS to GET it DONE:
_____   ☐ _____
_____   ☐ _____
_____   ☐ _____

DAY 2 / date: _____
VOLUNTEER / CHARITY IDEA: _____
WEBSITE / CONTACT: _____
HOW CAN I HELP?   STEPS to GET it DONE:
_____   ☐ _____
_____   ☐ _____
_____   ☐ _____

DAY 3 / date: _____
VOLUNTEER / CHARITY IDEA: _____
WEBSITE / CONTACT: _____
HOW CAN I HELP?   STEPS to GET it DONE:
_____   ☐ _____
_____   ☐ _____
_____   ☐ _____

DAY 4 / date: _____
VOLUNTEER / CHARITY IDEA: _____
WEBSITE / CONTACT: _____
HOW CAN I HELP?   STEPS to GET it DONE:
_____   ☐ _____
_____   ☐ _____
_____   ☐ _____

DAY 5 / date: _____
VOLUNTEER / CHARITY IDEA: _____
WEBSITE / CONTACT: _____
HOW CAN I HELP?   STEPS to GET it DONE:
_____   ☐ _____
_____   ☐ _____
_____   ☐ _____

DAYS 6-7 / date: _____
VOLUNTEER / CHARITY IDEA: _____
WEBSITE / CONTACT: _____
HOW CAN I HELP?   STEPS to GET it DONE:
_____   ☐ _____
_____   ☐ _____
_____   ☐ _____

a week of
DRAWING
PORTRAITS

NO MATTER HOW SKILLED YOU ARE at DRAWING, YOU CAN DRAW PORTRAITS! THE MAIN THING to FOCUS ON IS the SHAPE OF the HEAD and FEATURES. ARE the EYES CLOSE TOGETHER? IS the NOSE WIDE and FLAT? IS IT LONG and NARROW? IS their HEAD MORE OVAL-SHAPED OR IS IT MORE RECTANGULAR? JUST TAKE IT ONE SHAPE at a TIME. AND ≡DON'T WORRY≡, the WEIRDNESS and IMPERFECTIONS ARE WHAT MAKES it (YOUR OWN) COOL STYLE! EACH DAY CHOOSE EITHER a FAMILY MEMBER, FRIEND, OR FAMOUS PERSON (CURRENT OR HISTORIC) and DRAW them ANY WAY YOU WANT. YOU CAN DRAW the SAME PERSON EACH DAY to KEEP PRACTICING their FACIAL FEATURES- OR PICK a NEW PERSON EACH DAY.

THINGS to TAKE NOTICE of:

how does the hair frame the face? widow's peak? side part? curls?

is the head shape long and narrow? or more rounded?

are the eyebrows arched or flat and straight?

are the eyes opened wide or sort of squinty?

do the ears stick out or do they lay close to the head?

is the nose pointy or round and full?

DAY 2 / date: _____
PORtRAit OF: _____

DAY 1 / date: _____
PORtRAit OF: _____

DAY 3 / date: _____
PORtRAit OF: _____

DAY 4 / date: _____
PORtRAit OF: _____

DAYS 6-7 / date: _____
PORtRAit OF: _____

DAY 5 / date: _____
PORtRAit OF: _____

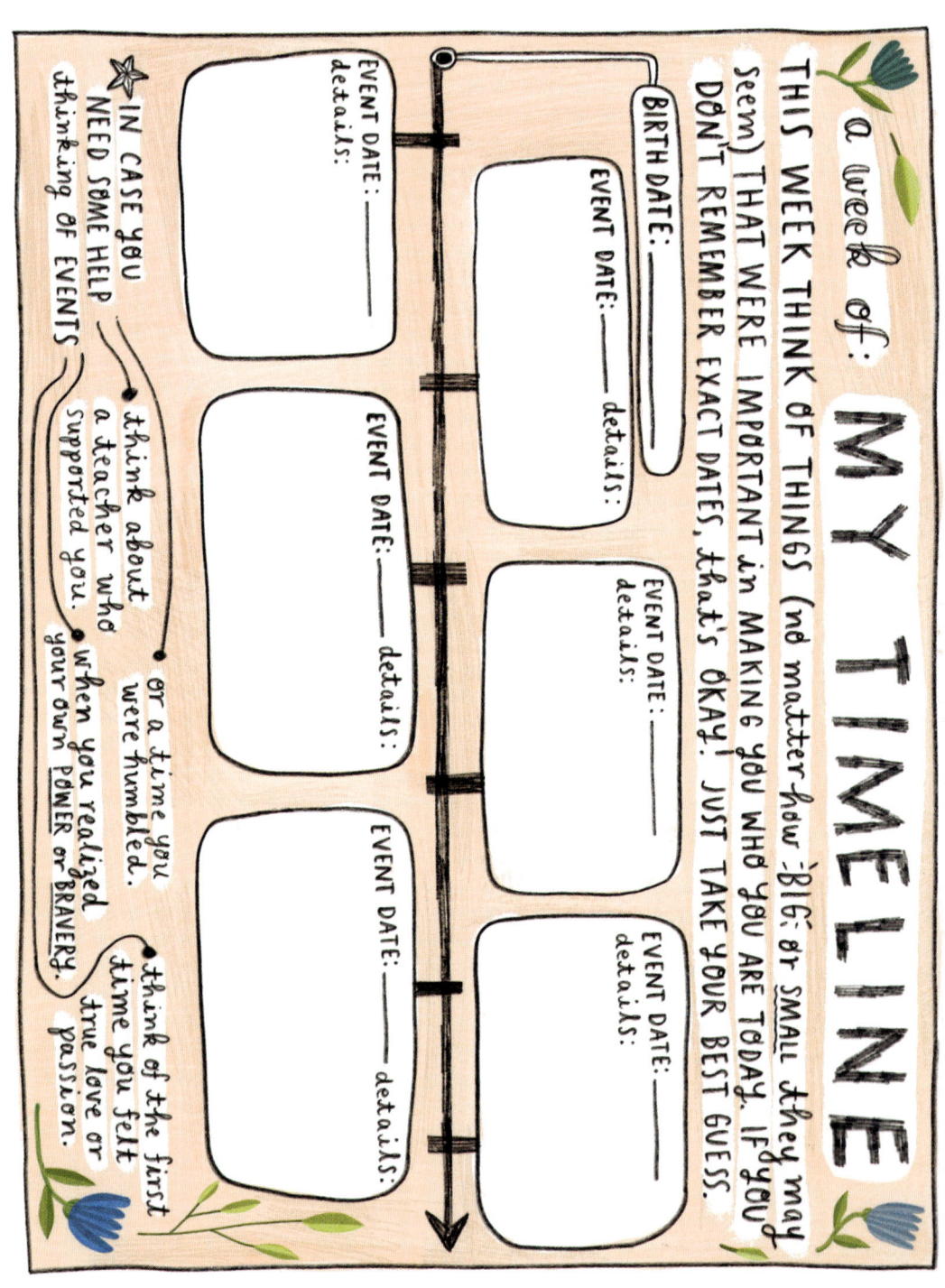

a week of: MY TIMELINE

THIS WEEK THINK OF THINGS (no matter how "BIG" or SMALL they may seem) THAT WERE IMPORTANT in MAKING you WHO YOU ARE TODAY. IF you DON'T REMEMBER EXACT DATES, that's OKAY! JUST TAKE YOUR BEST GUESS.

BIRTH DATE: _____

EVENT DATE: _____ details:

EVENT DATE: _____ details:

EVENT DATE: _____ details:

EVENT DATE: _____ details:

EVENT DATE: _____ details:

EVENT DATE: _____ details:

EVENT DATE: _____ details:

★ IN CASE you NEED SOME HELP thinking of EVENTS

• think about a teacher who supported you.

• or a time you were humbled.

• when you realized your own POWER or BRAVERY.

• think of the first time you felt true love or passion.

A WEEK OF BREATHING and RELAXATION practice

EXHALE

PRACTICE ONE of the RELAXATION or BREATHING EXERCISES EACH DAY. TAKE NOTES ABOUT HOW YOU FEEL THROUGHOUT the WEEK.

SOME BREATHING and RELAXATION TECHNIQUES and IDEAS

① TURN off the LIGHTS, LIGHT SOME CANDLES, and THINK of the THINGS that MADE YOU SMILE TODAY.

② LIE DOWN with YOUR EYES CLOSED. PLACE ONE HAND OVER YOUR HEART and the OTHER OVER YOUR BELLY. TAKE SLOW BREATHS, FOCUSING on the RISE and FALL of YOUR BELLY.

③ CLOSE YOUR EYES and IMAGINE YOUR FAVORITE PEACEFUL PLACE. IMAGINE YOU are THERE. ALLOW the PEACE to WASH OVER YOU.

④ SIT UP STRAIGHT, CLOSE YOUR EYES. REPEAT a MANTRA, FOR EXAMPLE "MY BODY is at PEACE," or "I DESERVE to FEEL HAPPINESS." REALLY FEEL the WORDS and ACKNOWLEDGE their TRUTH.

⑤ BEFORE BED, LIE DOWN FLAT, ARMS at YOUR SIDES. VISUALIZE EACH PART of YOUR BODY AS YOU RELAX it. START WITH YOUR TOES and MOVE UP YOUR WHOLE BODY, FOCUSING ON ONLY ONE PART at a TIME.

⑥ TAKE a WARM BATH OR SHOWER WITH YOUR BEST BATH SALTS OR BODY WASH. INHALE and EXHALE WHILE IMAGINING YOUR STRESS GOING RIGHT DOWN the DRAIN.

DAY 1

DATE:

_____

☐ BREATHING ☐ RELAXATION
TODAY I PRACTICED _____
_____
_____
_____
_____
_____
_____

DAY 2

DATE:

_____

☐ BREATHING ☐ RELAXATION
TODAY I PRACTICED _____
_____
_____
_____
_____
_____
_____

DAY 3

DATE:

_____

☐ BREATHING ☐ RELAXATION
TODAY I PRACTICED _____
_____
_____
_____
_____
_____
_____

DAY 4

DATE:

_____

☐ BREATHING ☐ RELAXATION
TODAY I PRACTICED _____
_____
_____
_____
_____
_____
_____

DAY 5

DATE:

_____

☐ BREATHING ☐ RELAXATION
TODAY I PRACTICED _____
_____
_____
_____
_____
_____
_____

DAYS 6-7

DATE:

_____

☐ BREATHING ☐ RELAXATION
TODAY I PRACTICED _____
_____
_____
_____
_____
_____

a WEEK OF LETTERING TIME

PRACTICE EACH STYLE of LETTERING.
WRITE the SAME WORD OVER and OVER
OR WRITE ANY WORDS YOU CHOOSE!

SOME OTHER IDEAS:

- PLAY with COLOR
- PLAY with LINE weight
- TRY WRITING YOUR NAME in EACH Style
- EXPERIMENT with PATTERNS

LET'S GO!

DAY 1/date: _____

BLOCKY LETTERS

HELLO

tip: AFTER DRAWING EACH LETTER SHAPE, DRAW SMALL LINES ALL GOING in the SAME DIRECTION FROM the CORNERS that WOULD SHOW UP IF TURNED to the SIDE.

THEN JUST CONNECT the LINES to MAKE it LOOK LIKE the SIDES of the LETTER.

* PRACTICE HERE ↗

DAY 2/date: _____

tip: FIRST WRITE
the WORD. then,
GO BACK and THICKEN
ALL LINES that
WERE WRITTEN in
A DOWNWARD
DIRECTION ↴

FANCY
hello

DAY 3/date: _____

tip: FIRST WRITE the
WORD LIGHTLY in PENCIL.

OFFICE TYPE
hello

① h

THEN, OUTLINE
the LETTER

② h

③ h   h ④

ERASE the
ORIGINAL LINES.

ADD the
LITTLE BAR
SHAPES to
the ENDS.

DAY 4/date: _____

tip: this ONE is VERY SIMILAR to DAY 3 — BUT this TIME ADD 2 POINTS GOING in OPPOSITE DIRECTIONS to the END OF EACH LINE.

FISHTAIL
hello

DAY 5/date: _____

tip: DRAW EACH PART OF the LETTERS with JAGGED ENDS

AFTER YOU DRAW ALL OF the LETTERS, GO BACK and FILL in with LITTLE LINES

WOODEN
HELLO

DAYS 6-7/date: _____

≥ YOU CHOOSE! ≤

TRY ONE (OR BOTH) OF these
LETTERING STYLES, PRACTICE
SOME FROM EARLIER this
WEEK, OR CREATE YOUR OWN!

POSITIVE/NEGATIVE

HELLO

tip: INSTEAD OF FILLING in
the LETTERS and LEAVING
the BACKGROUND BLANK,
DO the OPPOSITE.

ALL LINED UP

HELLO

tip: INSTEAD OF SINGLE LINES
FOR EACH PART OF the
LETTER, DRAW ③ LINES.

YAY! YOU ARE a LETTERING
PRO NOW!

A WEEK OF
PM ROUTINES

SETTING YOUR EVENING ROUTINE is JUST AS IMPORTANT AS YOUR MORNING ROUTINE. CREATE YOUR ROUTINES then STICK to them ALL WEEK!

Some ideas: BEDtime MEDitAtioN

BRUSH teeth   WASH FACE   PACK LUNCH

BREAthiNG EXERCISES   SEt out CLothes

WEEKDAYS:

PM ROUtiNE

WEEKENDS:

PM RoutiNE

DAY 1 / date: _____

☐ Routine Completed!

Notes: _____
_____
_____

DAY 2 / date: _____

☐ Routine Completed!

Notes: _____
_____
_____

DAY 3 / date: _____

☐ Routine Completed!

Notes: _____
_____
_____

DAY 4 / date: _____

☐ Routine Completed!

Notes: _____
_____
_____

DAY 5 / date: _____

☐ Routine Completed!

Notes: _____
_____
_____

DAYS 6-7 / date: _____

☐ Routine Completed!

Notes: _____
_____
_____

WHY STOP NOW?!

YOU DID IT!

KEEP IT UP!

A WEEK OF
GOALS

SETTING GOALS FOR YOURSELF, NO MATTER HOW LARGE or SMALL they ARE, CAN BE A WONDERFUL MOTIVATOR. DOING THINGS with AN OBJECTIVE in MIND HELPS to KEEP YOU FOCUSED and INTENTIONAL AS YOU WORK TOWARDS YOUR GOAL.

CHOOSE SOME GOALS (KEEP them ACHIEVABLE!) and FILL OUT the SHEETS on the NEXT PAGES. CUT them OUT and HANG them UP or CARRY them with YOU to HELP YOU KEEP ON TRACK.

G O A L S

GOAL: _____
GOAL DATE: _____ STEPS to COMPLETE:

☐ _____ ☐ _____
☐ _____ ☐ _____
☐ _____ ☐ _____
☐ _____ ☐ _____

GOAL: _____
GOAL DATE: _____ STEPS to COMPLETE:

☐ _____ ☐ _____
☐ _____ ☐ _____
☐ _____ ☐ _____
☐ _____ ☐ _____

GOAL: _____
GOAL DATE: _____ STEPS to COMPLETE:

☐ _____ ☐ _____
☐ _____ ☐ _____
☐ _____ ☐ _____
☐ _____ ☐ _____

DAY 1 / date: _____

DAY 2 / date: _____

DAY 3 / date: _____

GOALS

GOAL: _____
GOAL DATE: _____   **STEPS to COMPLETE:**

- ☐ _____   ☐ _____
- ☐ _____   ☐ _____
- ☐ _____   ☐ _____
- ☐ _____   ☐ _____

GOAL: _____
GOAL DATE: _____   **STEPS to COMPLETE:**

- ☐ _____   ☐ _____
- ☐ _____   ☐ _____
- ☐ _____   ☐ _____
- ☐ _____   ☐ _____

GOAL: _____
GOAL DATE: _____   **STEPS to COMPLETE:**

- ☐ _____   ☐ _____
- ☐ _____   ☐ _____
- ☐ _____   ☐ _____
- ☐ _____   ☐ _____

DAY 4 / date: _____

DAY 5 / date: _____

DAYS 6-7 / date: _____

I AM WORTH IT

I ROCK

GOAL CRUSHER

A WEEK OF
MEAL PLANNING

SPEND SOME TIME PLANNING YOUR DINNERS FOR NEXT WEEK. PLANNING AHEAD SAVES TIME, MAKES it EASIER to MAKE HEALTHY CHOICES, and it JUST FEELS GOOD to BE AHEAD OF the GAME!

ONCE YOU DECIDE WHAT to HAVE, ADD ANY INGREDIENTS YOU NEED to the LIST ON the NEXT PAGE.

DAY 1 / date: _____

DINNER FOR NEXT MONDAY
date: _____

WHAT I'M GOING to HAVE:
_____
_____
_____

WHERE I CAN FIND the RECIPE(S):
_____
_____
_____

☆ DON'T FORGET to ADD ANY INGREDIENTS YOU NEED to the SHOPPING LIST!

DAY 2 / date: _____

DINNER FOR NEXT TUESDAY
date: _____

WHAT I'M GOING to HAVE:
_____
_____
_____

WHERE I CAN FIND the RECIPE(S):
_____
_____
_____

☆ DON'T FORGET to ADD ANY INGREDIENTS YOU NEED to the SHOPPING LIST!

DAY 3 / date: _____

DINNER FOR NEXT WEDNESDAY
date: _____

WHAT I'M GOING to HAVE:
_____
_____
_____

WHERE I CAN FIND the
RECIPE(S): _____
_____
_____

☆ DON'T FORGET to ADD ANY
INGREDIENTS YOU NEED to
the SHOPPING LIST!

DAY 4 / date: _____

DINNER FOR NEXT THURSDAY
date: _____

WHAT I'M GOING to HAVE:
_____
_____
_____

WHERE I CAN FIND the
RECIPE(S): _____
_____
_____

☆ DON'T FORGET to ADD ANY
INGREDIENTS YOU NEED to
the SHOPPING LIST!

DAY 5 / date: _____

DINNER FOR NEXT FRIDAY
date: _____

WHAT I'M GOING to HAVE:
_____
_____
_____

WHERE I CAN FIND the
RECIPE(S): _____
_____
_____

☆ DON'T FORGET to ADD ANY
INGREDIENTS YOU NEED to
the SHOPPING LIST!

DAYS 6-7 / date: _____

DINNER FOR NEXT SATURDAY
date: _____

WHAT I'M GOING to HAVE:
_____
_____
_____

WHERE I CAN FIND the
RECIPE(S): _____
_____
_____

☆ DON'T FORGET to ADD ANY
INGREDIENTS YOU NEED to
the SHOPPING LIST!

SHOPPING LIST
_____ _____
_____ _____
_____ _____
_____ _____

A WEEK of SHOES

DRAW the SHOES YOU are WEARING EACH DAY. IF YOU tend to WEAR the SAME SHOES MOST DAYS, JUST DRAW LOTS of DIFFERENT SHOE STYLES!

DAY 1/date: _____

DAY 2/date: _____

DAY 3/date: _____

DAY 4/date: _____

DAY 5/date: _____

DAYS 6-7/date: _____

WHAT are POSITIVE AFFIRMATIONS?

POSITIVE AFFIRMATIONS are PHRASES or STATEMENTS that YOU REPEAT to YOURSELF to ENCOURAGE POSITIVE CHANGE, SELF-LOVE, and INCREASED CONFIDENCE.

this week you'll pick some affirmations to start implementing into your daily life. Choose 2-3 from the list on the next page or create some of your own. Once you've decided on your affirmations, you'll use the log sheet to track your progress and any notes you'd like to add along the way.

I AM CUNNING and SMART and CAN EVADE EVEN the EARLIEST EARLY BIRD.

I WILL WAKE UP ENERGIZED and ALERT and WILL BE the EARLIEST EARLY BIRD.

POSITIVE AFFIRMATIONS

I GET to DECIDE MY OWN LIFE'S PATH.

I AM CAPABLE OF FULFILLING MY DREAMS.

CHALLENGES ALLOW ME to BE REMINDED of MY OWN RESILIENCE.

I DO NOT LET the NEGATIVITY of OTHERS BECOME MY OWN.

I CAN STAND UP FOR MYSELF and MY BELIEFS and I DON'T NEED to APOLOGIZE FOR DOING SO.

I AM A KIND and LOYAL FRIEND and DESERVE to HAVE the SAME in RETURN.

MY BODY IS STRONG, CAPABLE, and IT IS WORTH TAKING CARE of.

I AM NOT OBLIGATED to SAY "YES" to EVERY REQUEST and CAN CONFIDENTLY SAY "NO" WHEN I NEED to.

MY AFFIRMATIONS

1. _____
   _____
   _____

2. _____
   _____
   _____

3. _____
   _____
   _____

- SET ASIDE ABOUT 5 MINUTES, 3 TIMES EACH DAY. SET A REMINDER *if* IT WILL HELP YOU REMEMBER.

- TAKE A FEW DEEP BREATHS *and* REPEAT EACH PHRASE SLOWLY, 3-5 TIMES. REALLY FEEL *the* <u>POWER</u> *and* <u>TRUTH</u> OF YOUR WORDS AS YOU SAY *them*. THEN, TAKE A FEW MORE DEEP, INTENTIONAL BREATHS AS YOU DECIDE *to* MAINTAIN *this* POSITIVITY THROUGHOUT YOUR DAY.

LET'S *get* STARTED

AFFIRMATION TRACKER

DAY 1 / date:

☐ #1 ☐ #2
☐ #3

NOTES (HOW DID I FEEL DURING/AFTER/ FOR the REMAINDER of the DAY?): _____
_____
_____
_____

DAY 2 / date:

☐ #1 ☐ #2
☐ #3

NOTES (HOW DID I FEEL DURING/AFTER/ FOR the REMAINDER of the DAY?): _____
_____
_____
_____

DAY 3 / date:

☐ #1 ☐ #2
☐ #3

NOTES (HOW DID I FEEL DURING/AFTER/ FOR the REMAINDER of the DAY?): _____
_____
_____
_____

DAY 4 / date:

☐ #1 ☐ #2
☐ #3

NOTES (HOW DID I FEEL DURING/AFTER/ FOR the REMAINDER of the DAY?): _____
_____
_____
_____

DAY 5 / date:

☐ #1 ☐ #2
☐ #3

NOTES (HOW DID I FEEL DURING/AFTER/ FOR the REMAINDER of the DAY?): _____
_____
_____
_____

DAYS 6-7 / date:

☐ #1 ☐ #2
☐ #3

NOTES (HOW DID I FEEL DURING/AFTER/ FOR the REMAINDER of the DAY?): _____
_____
_____
_____

a week of: **CURRENT FAVES** FOR THE YEAR _____
(CURRENT YEAR)

MAKE LISTS of YOUR CURRENT TOP 3 FAVORITE things to LOOK BACK ON in the FUTURE!

DAY 1/date: _____
TOP 3 FAVE PLACES
① _____
② _____
③ _____

DAY 2/date: _____
TOP 3 FAVE SHOWS
① _____
② _____
③ _____

DAY 3/date:_____ TOP 3 FAVE WEBSITES.
(blogs/news sites/DIY sites...)
① _____ ② _____
③ _____

DAY 4/date:_____
TOP 3 FAVE SPARE
TIME ACTIVITIES.
① _____
② _____
③ _____

DAY 5/date:_____
TOP 3 FAVE SONGS
① _____
② _____
③ _____

DAYS 6-7/date:_____
TOP 3 FAVE RESTAURANTS
① _____
② _____
③ _____

HOWARD'S
hot dogs

OPEN

A WEEK OF RUGS

DESIGN the RUGS YOU'D LOVE to SEE ON YOUR FLOORS!

DAY 1 / date: _____

DAY 2/ date: _____

DAY 3/ date: _____

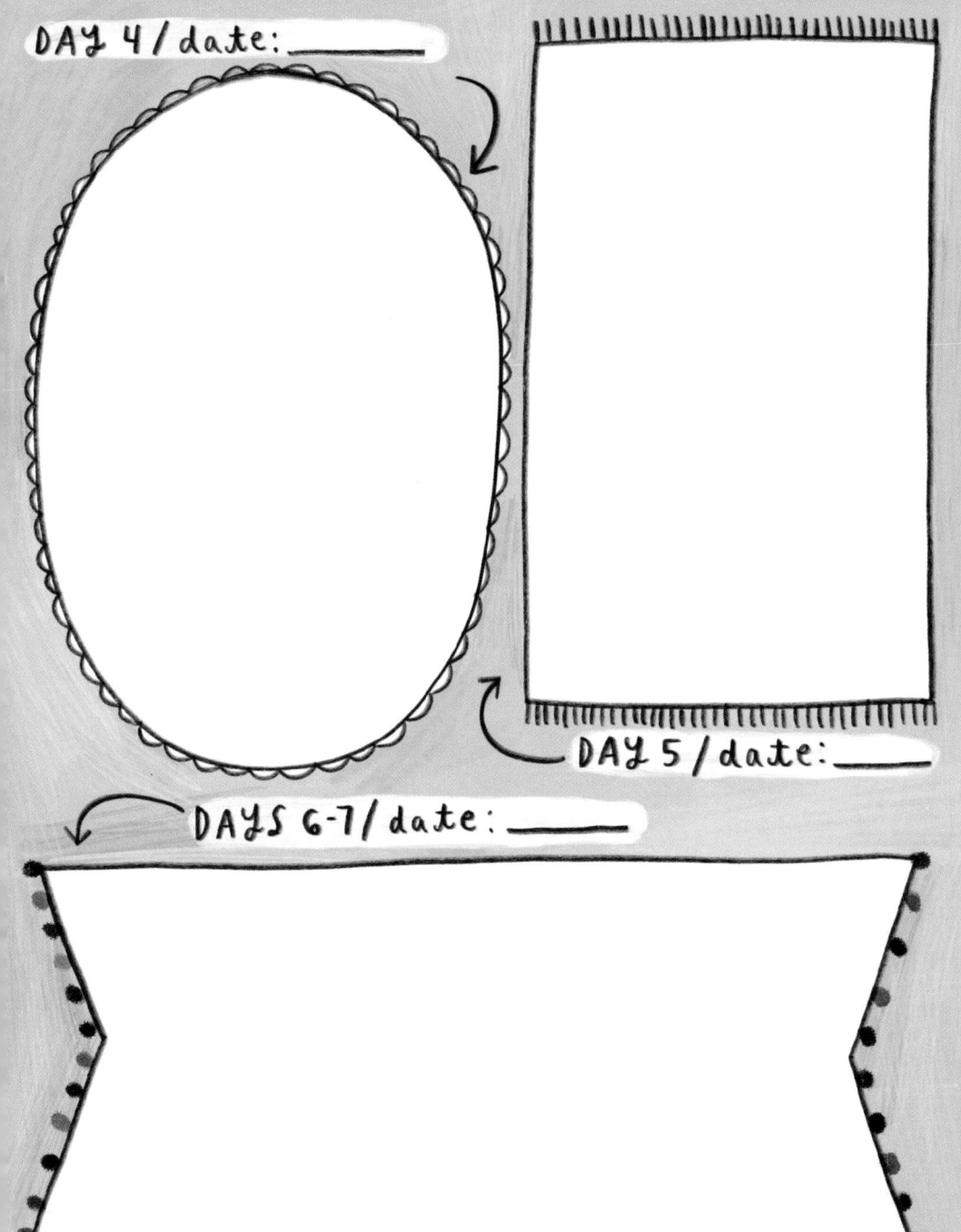

DAY 4 / date:_____

DAY 5 / date:_____

DAYS 6-7 / date:_____

a week of:

Learning a New Language

SALAAM

olá

SHIKAMOO

CIAO

BONJOUR

SHALOM

merhaba

KONNICHIWA

CHOOSE A LANGUAGE from the LIST BELOW or A DIFFERENT ONE that YOU'RE INTERESTED in LEARNING. EACH DAY YOU'LL BE ONE STEP CLOSER to BECOMING FLUENT in a WHOLE NEW WAY of COMMUNICATING!

SWAHILI   SPANISH   ARABIC   GERMAN   SWEDISH
PORTUGUESE   HINDI   CROATIAN   FRENCH
RUSSIAN   ITALIAN   DUTCH   ROMANIAN

I CHOSE: _____

DAY 1/date: _____

HELLO: ① _____

② _____

③ _____

HOW DO YOU SAY, "HELLO" IN the LANGUAGE YOU CHOSE? WRITE it 3 TIMES. THEN, DRAW the FLAG of a COUNTRY that COMMONLY SPEAKS this LANGUAGE.

LEARN how to TELL SOMEONE YOUR NAME and WRITE it 3 TIMES.

DAY 2/date: _____

① _____

② _____

③ _____

ME LLAMO _____.

LEARNING NUMBERS   DAY 3/ date: _____

WRITE EACH NUMBER three TIMES

1 _____ **2** _____ **3** _____
_____ _____ _____
_____ _____ _____

DAY 4/ date: _____   **COLORS**

FIND OUT HOW to SAY and WRITE
the COLORS, then WRITE them THREE TIMES.

YELLOW _____ _____ _____

PINK _____ _____ _____

BLUE _____ _____ _____

LOVE   DAY 5/ date: _____

LEARN how to SAY "I LOVE YOU" and WRITE IT THREE TIMES.

① _____

② _____   ③ _____

DAYS 6-7/ date: _____
FIND OUT how to SAY ⟶   **I AM BEAUTIFUL!**
and WRITE it THREE TIMES.

① _____

② _____   ③ _____

WHY STOP NOW?! KEEP LEARNING! THERE are SO MANY
FREE ONLINE RESOURCES to HELP YOU BECOME FLUENT
in the LANGUAGE YOU'VE BEEN LEARNING this WEEK.

A WEEK of

HELPING OTHERS

HELP with CARRYING GROCERIES

BRING DINNER to A FRIEND or NEIGHBOR GOING THROUGH A HARD time.

MOW the GRASS or TAKE OUT the TRASH for A NEIGHBOR.

HELP A FAMILY MEMBER RUN ERRANDS.

OFFER to HELP OUT AROUND the HOUSE.

BABYSit WHEN YOU SEE A FRIEND in A PINCH.

WHAT ARE SOME things YOU CAN DO to HELP A FRIEND, NEIGHBOR, FAMILY MEMBER, or EVEN A COMPLETE STRANGER? IT DOESN't HAVE to BE SOMETHING BIG — EVEN the SMALLEST GESTURES CAN MAKE A DIFFERENCE to SOMEONE in NEED. TRY to HELP at LEAST ONE PERSON EACH DAY.

DAY 1 / date: _____
WHO I HELPED: _____
WHAT I DID: _____
_____
_____
_____
_____

DAY 2 / date: _____
WHO I HELPED: _____
WHAT I DID: _____
_____
_____
_____
_____

DAY 3 / date: _____
WHO I HELPED: _____
WHAT I DID: _____
_____
_____
_____
_____

DAY 4 / date: _____
WHO I HELPED: _____
WHAT I DID: _____
_____
_____
_____
_____

DAY 5 / date: _____
WHO I HELPED: _____
WHAT I DID: _____
_____
_____
_____
_____

DAYS 6-7 / date: _____
WHO I HELPED: _____
WHAT I DID: _____
_____
_____
_____
_____

a week of

BUGS

PICK SOME BUGS FROM the LIST BELOW (or CHOOSE YOUR OWN!) to RESEARCH and DRAW. PLAY and EXPERIMENt with DIFFERENT COLORS and MEDIUMS: PEN, PENCIL, MARKER, COLORED PENCILS, GOUACHE, or ANYthING ELSE YOU HAVE on HAND!

honey bee   june bug   giant dragonfly
green scarab beetle   wood ant   leaf cricket
hawk moth   long horned beetle   sand wasp

DAY 1 / date: _____

INSECT NAME: _____

GRASShOPPER

DAY 2 / date: _____

INSECT NAME: _____

YELLOW JACKEt

DAY 3/date: _____

INSECT NAME: _____

← ANt

DAY 4/date: _____

INSECT NAME: _____

DAY 5/date: _____

INSECT NAME: _____

DAYS 6-7/date: _____

STAG BEETLE

INSECT NAME: _____

A WEEK OF RECIPES

THIS WEEK is ALL ABOUT FINDING RECIPES YOU WANT to TRY. IF YOU AREN't A SUPER GREAT COOK, that's OKAY! LOOK UP SIMPLE RECIPES FOR BEGINNERS. IF YOU ALSO WANT to MAKE them this WEEK, (GO for it!) OTHERWISE, SAVE them FOR WHEN YOU'RE in the MOOD to TRY SOMETHING NEW!

RECIPE NAME:

WHERE I GOT IT:

INGREDIENTS:

Recipe Name

WHERE I GOT IT:

INGREDIENTS:

RECIPE NAME:

WHERE I GOT IT:

INGREDIENTS:

DIRECTIONS

DIRECTIONS

DIRECTIONS

DAY 4/date: _____

recipe name: _____

WHERE I GOT IT: _____

INGREDIENTS:

_____
_____
_____
_____
_____
_____
_____
_____

DAY 5/date: _____

RECIPE NAME _____

WHERE I GOT IT: _____

INGREDIENTS:

_____
_____
_____
_____
_____
_____
_____
_____

DAYS 6-7/date: _____

RECIPE NAME _____

WHERE I GOT IT: _____

INGREDIENTS:

_____
_____
_____
_____
_____
_____
_____
_____

DIRECTIONS

DIRECTIONS

DIRECTIONS

A WEEK OF *Gratitude*

FEELING THANKFUL for the THINGS WE HAVE in OUR LIVES CAN FILL US with A SENSE OF PEACE, CONTENTMENT, and APPRECIATION. With PRACTICE, we CAN LEARN to CARRY those POSITIVE FEELINGS with US ALMOST ALL of the TIME.

THINK ABOUT these QUESTIONS this WEEK:

→ WHAT ARE SOME LITTLE things that BRING YOU JOY?

→ WHAT ARE SOME THINGS that MAKE YOU SMILE?

→ WHAT is SOMEthing YOU FEEL LUCKY to HAVE EXPERIENCED?

DAY 1 / date: _____ — DRAW them or WRITE the REASONS YOU ARE GRATEFUL FOR them.

SOMEONE I AM GRATEFUL FOR:

DAY 2 / date: _____ — DRAW it or WRITE the REASONS YOU ARE GRATEFUL FOR it.

SOMEthing SMALL I'M GRATEFUL FOR:

DAY 3 / date: _____ — DRAW it or WRITE the REASONS YOU ARE GRATEFUL FOR it.

SOMEthing ELSE I'M GRATEFUL FOR:

DAY 4/ date: _____

SOMETHING I'M GRATEFUL I'M ABLE to DO:

DRAW or WRITE the REASONS YOU ARE GRATEFUL FOR it.

DAY 5/ date: _____

SOMETHING I'M GRATEFUL to HAVE DONE:

DRAW or WRITE the REASONS YOU ARE GRATEFUL FOR it.

DAYS 6-7/ date: _____

SOMETHING NON-TANGIBLE I AM THANKFUL FOR:

DRAW or WRITE the REASONS YOU ARE GRATEFUL FOR it.

EACH DAY TRY to TAKE TIME to THINK ABOUT A FEW THINGS YOU ARE GRATEFUL FOR.

FAMILY and FRIENDS

COFFEE!

FLOWERS

LOVE.

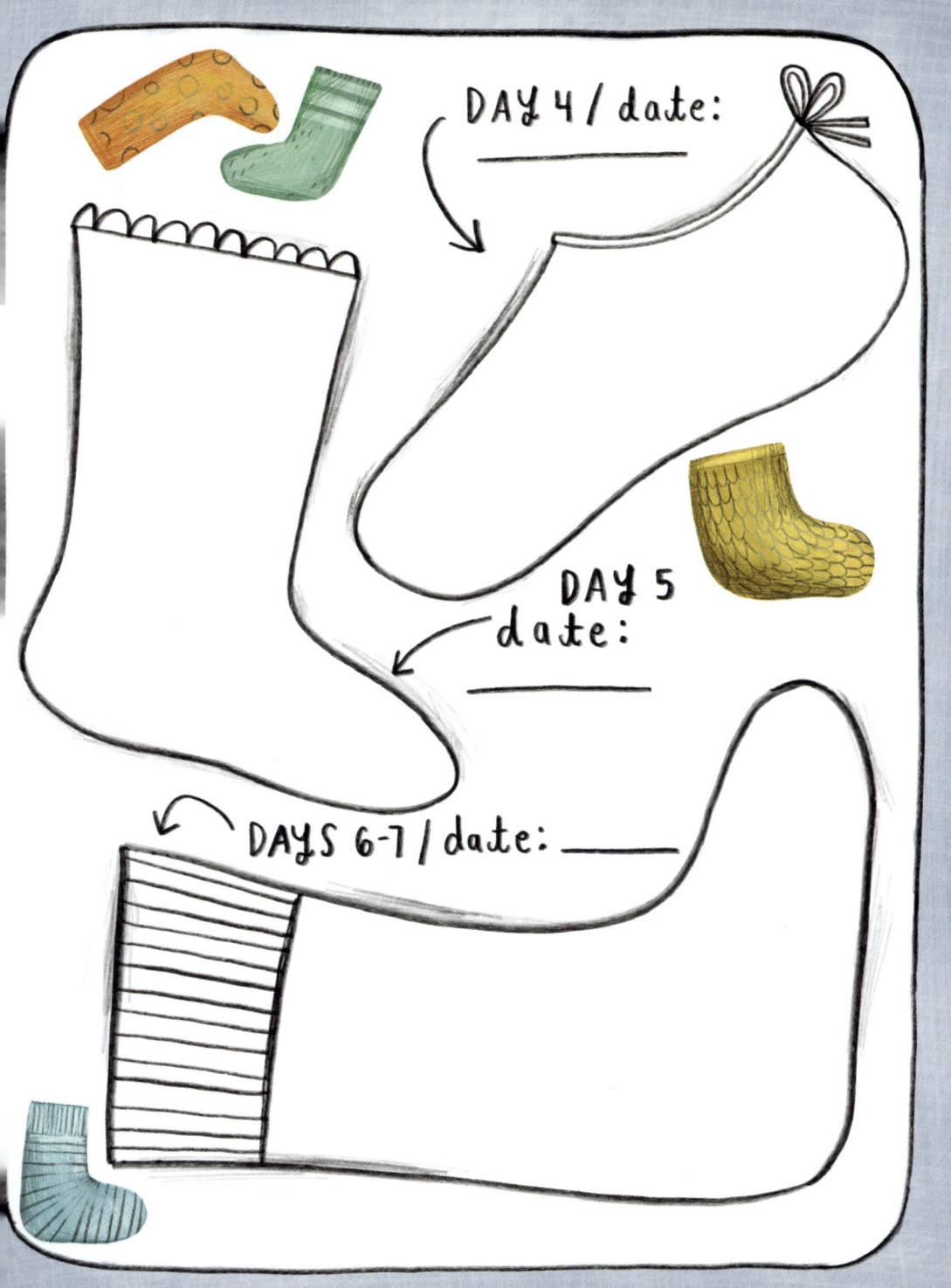

DAY 4 / date: _____

DAY 5
date: _____

DAYS 6-7 / date: _____

A WEEK OF Still life DRAWINGS

STILL LIFE DRAWINGS ARE JUST DRAWINGS of THINGS that ARE in FRONT OF YOU. YOU CAN PiCK ANYTHING— A VASE of FLOWERS, YOUR GLASSES, A LAMP, BOOKS... WHATEVER is AROUND YOU CAN BE DRAWN. DON't WORRY ABOUT MAKiNG it PERFECT - JUST HAVE A GOOD TIME. SOMEtiMES the WONKY and ODD PARTS ARE WHAT MAKE the <u>COOLESt ARt</u>!

PICK A NEW OBJECT (or OBJECTS) EACH DAY to DRAW. MODIFY YOUR LEVEL of DETAiL DEPENDiNG ON how MUCH TIME YOU HAVE EACH DAY.

DAY 1 / date: _____

DAY 2 / date: _____

DAY 3/ date: _____

DAY 4/ date: _____

DAY 5/ date: _____

DAYS 6-7/ date: _____

A WEEK OF

NOTE WRITING

THIS WEEK is ALL ABOUT REMINDING YOUR FRIENDS and FAMILY HOW AMAZING they ARE!

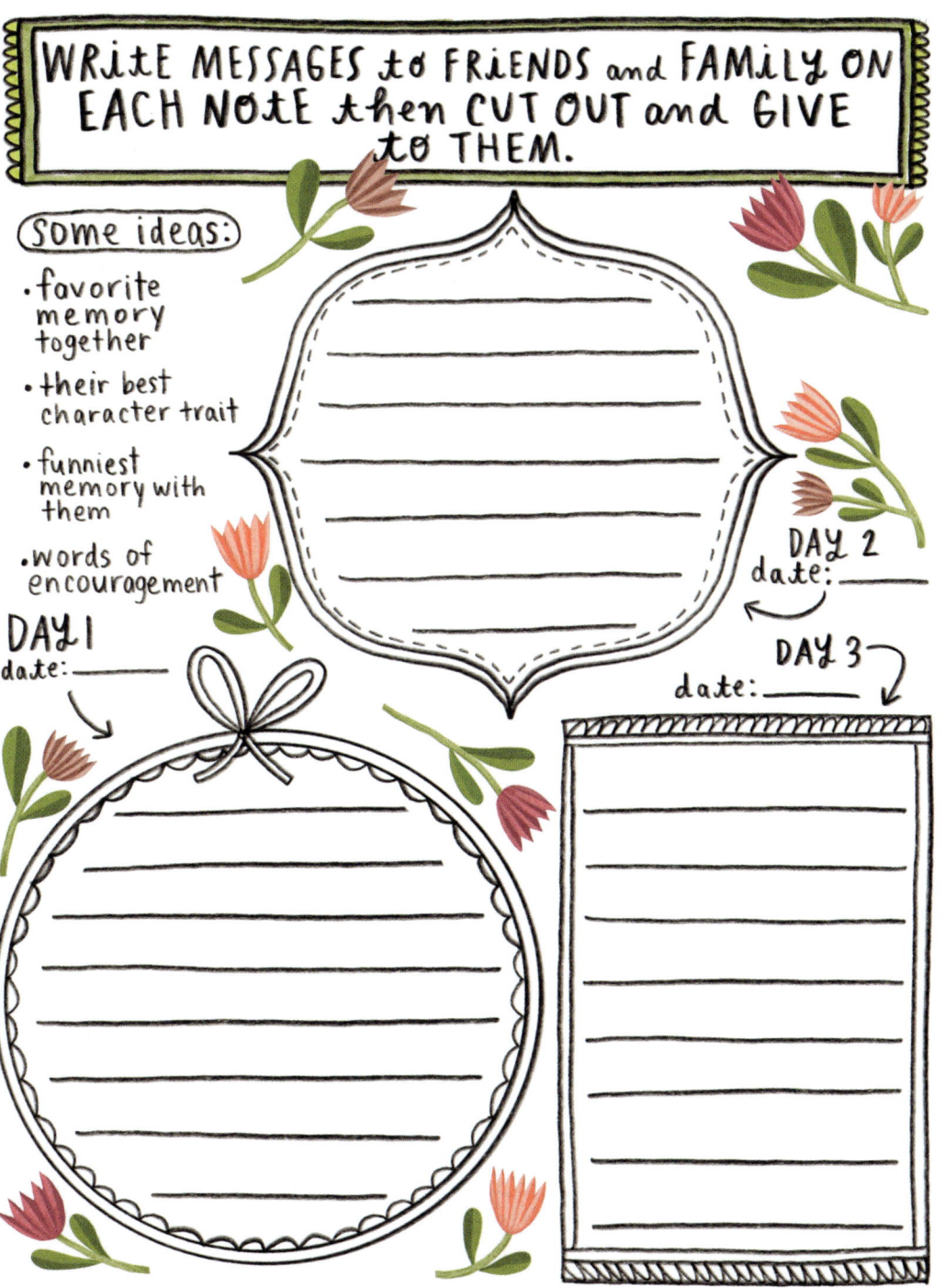

WRITE MESSAGES to FRIENDS and FAMILY ON EACH NOTE then CUT OUT and GIVE to THEM.

Some ideas:

- favorite memory together
- their best character trait
- funniest memory with them
- words of encouragement

DAY 1
date:_____

DAY 2
date:_____

DAY 3
date:_____

DAY 4/date: _____

DAY 5/date: _____

DAYS 6-7/date _____

A WEEK OF ALL-TIME FAVE FOODS

DAY 1/date: _____
FAVORITE (JUNK FOOD)

DAY 2/date: _____
FAVORITE (BEVERAGE)

DAY 4/date: _____
FAVORITE (FRUIT/VEGGIE)

DAY 3/date: _____
FAVORITE (BREAKFAST)

DAY 5/date: _____
FAVORITE (DESSERT)

DAYS 6-7/date: _____
FAVORITE (HEALTH FOOD)

A WEEK OF SPENDING LESS MONEY

IT'S COMPLETELY POSSIBLE to SAVE MONEY JUST BY CUTTING a FEW THINGS Out of YOUR ROUTINE at a TIME. THINK of SOME things YOU CAN DO to BEGIN SAVING this WEEK.

HERE are SOME ideas to GET YOU started:

- TAKE PUBLIC TRANSPORTATION
- MAKE COFFEE AT HOME
- BRING LUNCHES TO WORK
- FIND FREE EVENTS IN YOUR AREA
- MAKE GIFTS / CARDS
- CANCEL UNUSED SUBSCRIPTION SERVICES

- SHOP AT CONSIGNMENT STORES
- DON'T PAY WITH A CREDIT CARD
- ONLY BUY WHAT'S ON YOUR SHOPPING LIST
- HOST A POTLUCK INSTEAD OF A PRICEY NIGHT OUT
- BUY GENERIC BRANDS

- CARRY A FEW SNACKS WITH YOU INSTEAD OF BUYING THEM

SHOPPING LIST
- ☑ kiwis
- ☑ bell pepper
- ☑ bread
- ☐ cheese
- ☐ salmon

CITY TRANSPORT

EACH DAY WRITE DOWN WHAT YOU DID to SAVE YOURSELF MONEY. GO ON... Start Saving!

DAY/date	WHAT I DID to SAVE	APROXIMATE SAVINGS #
DAY 1 date:		
DAY 2 date:		
DAY 3 date:		
DAY 4 date:		
DAY 5 date:		
DAYS 6-7 date:		

a week of

ME

WHAT ARE YOUR TEETH SHAPED LIKE?

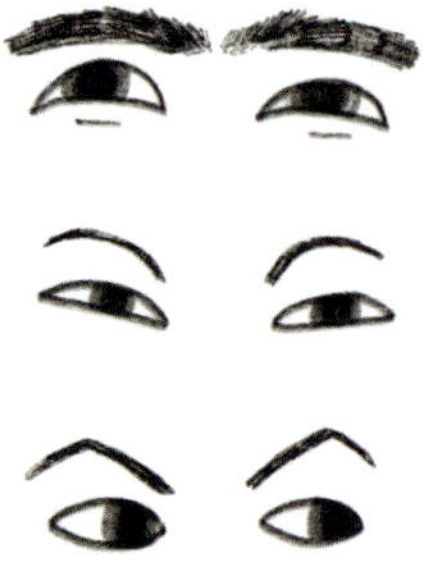

HOW ARE YOUR EYEBROWS SHAPED?

this week you'll create a self-portrait! Don't worry - it doesn't need to be perfect and you have all week to work on it. Just focus on the shapes of each feature, one at a time... you can ≡totally≡ do this!

WHAT HEAD SHAPE DO YOU HAVE?

SQUARE-ISH?

ROUND?

OVAL?

EYE SHAPE?

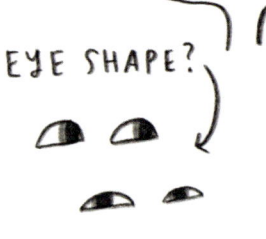

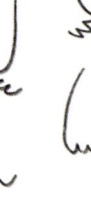

WHAT is YOUR NOSE LIKE?

HOW ABOUT YOUR LIPS?

WEEK of: _____

HERE I AM in ALL of MY AMAZING,
BEAUTIFUL, UNIQUE, TALENTED, CREATIVE,
INCREDIBLE GLORY!

SERIOUSLY... YOU ARE
AMAZING

YOU'VE DONE it!

I REALLY HOPE YOU'RE AS PROUD OF YOU AS I AM. YOU'VE STRETCHED YOURSELF CREATIVELY, EMOTIONALLY, GONE OUT OF YOUR COMFORT ZONE, HELPED OTHERS, and SO MANY OTHER FABULOUS things! JUST BECAUSE the BOOK is FINISHED that DOESN'T MEAN YOUR JOURNEY HAS to END HERE! GO BACK through and FIND YOUR FAVORITE WEEKS, JOT them DOWN ON the NEXT PAGE and ...

KEEP YOUR ADVENTURE GOING!

XOXO, —erica

MY VERY FAVORITE WEEKS.

TOPIC	WHY I LOVED IT	HOW I CAN KEEP IT GOING

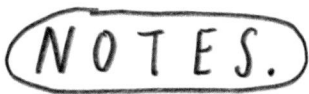

NOTES.

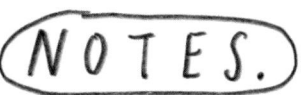

NOTES.

NOTES.